S

TAKING CARE OF BUSINESS

STORIES OF CANADIAN
WOMEN ENTREPRENEURS

Also by Heather Robertson

Non-fiction

Reservations Are for Indians

Grass Roots

Salt of the Earth

A Terrible Beauty: The Art of Canada at War

The Flying Bandit

More than a Rose: Prime Ministers, Wives and Other Women

On the Hill: A People's Guide to Canada's Parliament

Driving Force: The McLaughlin Family and the Age of the Car

Fiction

Willie: A Romance

Lily, a Rhapsody in Red

Igor, a Novel of Intrigue

Anthologies

Her Own Woman

Canada's Newspapers: The Inside Story

From the Country

Edited

A Gentleman Adventurer: The Arctic Diaries of Richard Bonnycastle

I Fought Riel, by Major Charles Boulton

TAKING CARE OF BUSINESS

STORIES OF CANADIAN
WOMEN ENTREPRENEURS

EDITED BY
HEATHER ROBERTSON

First published in Canada in 1997 by
Fenn Publishing Company Ltd.
34 Nixon Road
Bolton, Ontario
Canada L7E 1W2

Canadian Cataloguing in Publication Data

Main entry under title:

Taking care of business : Stories of Canadian
    Women Entrepreneurs

ISBN 1-55168-104-8

1. Businesswomen – Canada. 2. Women-owned business
enterprises – Canada.   3. Entrepreneurship – Canada.
I. Robertson, Heather, 1942–   .

HD6072.6.C2T34 1997   338'.04'092271   C97-931106-3

TABLE OF CONTENTS

COPYRIGHT ACKNOWLEDGEMENTS

ACKNOWLEDGEMENTS

This book would not have been possible without the generous co-operation of the women profiled, who took hours from their busy schedules to discuss details of their businesses and their personal lives. Thanks too to our writers for their extra effort and care, and to the organizers and sponsors of the "Canadian Woman Entrepreneur of the Year" awards and conference. The 1996 conference gave me insight into the world of women in business, the opportunity to hear many wonderful stories, and the chance to meet some of the outstanding women profiled in this book.

Taking Care of Business was inspired by Sue Chaiton, and polished by copy editor Wendy Thomas.

INTRODUCTION
TAKING CARE OF BUSINESS

Welcome to the wild, wacky, and profitable world of women in business! *Taking Care of Business* introduces you to twenty successful Canadian women who own and run their own businesses. They come from all walks of life, and they sell everything from butter to biochemicals. Not all of these women are millionaires — yet — and it may surprise you to find out that not one of them is in it only for the money.

A few of these women are partners, working together to build joint enterprises, others are loners. They are married and single, mothers, grandmothers, or childless by choice, and they range in age from their mid-thirties to mid-seventies. You will meet women who jumped into business a few years ago, and others who grew up ringing a cash register. They live in cities, towns, and remote areas scattered across the country, from the isolated outport of Ship Cove, Newfoundland, to Whitehorse, Yukon.

These women are remarkable, but not unique or exceptional: we could have chosen a different twenty or made room for dozens more. Some names you will recognize; others you will never have heard before. Thousands of women in Canada are running successful businesses, large and small, high profile and obscure. As a freelance writer, I am an entrepreneur, and so are all the writers who contributed to this book. Novelist Margaret Atwood recently incorporated her own company, O.W. Toad, and in 1979, my then publisher's sales rep in Calgary, Keri Longpré, quit her job to start Sandpiper Books with two women partners. In Toronto, two charismatic women, Beth Appeldoorn and Susan Sandler, founded Longhouse, a legendary bookstore that made CanLit respectable and, later, famous. There's no such thing as a "woman's business": Angela Lisi, owner of American Sound in Richmond Hill, Ontario, has been selling audio equipment, almost exclusively to men, since 1989.

Businesswomen tend to be depicted as Valkyries in steel-toed boots or bored socialites dabbling in tweaky boutiques. A broad definition of entrepreneur also includes corporate executives, even when these women are cogs in male-dominated multinationals or partners in companies founded and owned by men. Some daughters inherit a corporation from Dad or enough money to start one. How could we choose?

We decided to look for women who have built their own businesses from scratch or who have transformed a marginal concern into a dynamic enterprise. We wanted nitty-gritty, hands-on business experience: women who have put up their own money, taken the risks, done the work, and made the decisions, women who are still actively running their businesses and who are unequivocally The Boss.

The women you will meet here are also good storytellers. They talk frankly about the nuts and bolts of their businesses, the difficulties of getting started, their triumphs and disasters, the stresses on their families and personal lives. Some have come back from the brink of bankruptcy; others have persevered through chronic illness, separation, divorce, and the sudden death of a partner. Their hair-raising, heart-warming stories are full of wise, practical advice for women of all ages who are already in business, or who are thinking of taking the plunge.

Where do you begin? Business is unknown territory for most women. Fifty years ago, we were supposed to stay home and raise kids; twenty-five years ago, we were urged to get a job. Now those jobs are evaporating. Career women are being downsized, and for many young women, jobs don't exist. The only alternative may be to create a job for ourselves. Sounds great, but how do we do it? And what if we fail?

Let's be realistic. Women suffer from a number of handicaps. A big one is lack of money, and our first problem is psychological. For generations, we have been told that women "don't have a head for business" or "girls can't do math" or "it isn't ladylike to talk about money." Women who take charge of the family finances are accused of "wearing the pants," if they are allowed to take charge at all.

Until recently, women rarely owned property, and, if they married, they became their husband's property. Farms and estates were left to male relatives, on whom women became dependent, or were placed in the charge of banks or trustees. Husbands were free to dispose of their wives' inheritances. Single women who worked for wages were forced to quit their jobs when they married; it was assumed that married women belonged at home, rewarded, if they were lucky, with a meagre monthly allowance from their husbands. When Canada's Family Allowance, paid directly to mothers, was introduced in 1944, those cheques were the first money of their own many women had ever seen.

It's not a big surprise, then, that women who would like to go into business are often intimidated by financial issues. How much money do they need? Where are they going to get it? What if they lose it?

A capital investment is necessary to start any business, whether the amount is $1,000 or $100,000: there are supplies and equipment to buy, phones to install, taxes and rent to pay, transportation costs, and — the last thing many women think about — the cost of their own time and labour. Many women stake their savings, or a cash buy-out from a job severance, and many are able to borrow from family or friends. Banks will lend start-up money, but only if you have enough assets — savings, bonds, RSPs, or real estate — to guarantee the loan. Going into business, therefore, isn't a realistic option for single mothers on welfare or unemployed youth.

The up-side for women entrepreneurs is that once they get started in business, women are twice as likely as men to succeed! A 1984 Ontario study by Jerry White, "The Rise of Female Capitalism," found that women do better because they have more modest expectations, do more research, and aren't afraid to ask for advice. They also support each other, and provide jobs for other women. It's not surprising, therefore, that of the 150,000 new businesses started each year in Canada, more than half are created by women, and women are active in all areas of business ownership, including trucking, agriculture, and tourism, as well as the more traditional areas of food services, retail clothing, and interior design. Is there anything a woman entrepreneur won't tackle, and can't do?

Of course, women have been taking care of business since we began trading eggs, vegetables, and moccasins for iron kettles and other home improvements. Farm women have traditionally kept the books and balanced the budgets; many urban women run their households like corporate CEOs, play the stock market, and invest profitably in real estate. A surprising number of women we interviewed for *Taking Care of Business* had mothers or other female relatives who sold products, managed hotels, or opened shops to augment their husbands' incomes. In my own mother's family, my grandmother was the financial whiz. A good thing too, or they would have starved. Much of the tragedy of elderly widows living in poverty can be traced directly to their husbands' inept and irresponsible handling of money.

Okay, so you've got some cash to put on the line, and a skill or a product you think you can sell. What's next? Buy a ton of stuff? Rent a storefront? Hang up a sign? Phone all your friends? Take out an ad?

If you plan to survive, the next step is to ask questions. Who is going to buy what I have to sell, and will they pay me enough to make it worth my while? Research the market. Call your chamber of commerce, board of trade, or the government department that regulates your area of interest. Who is your competition? How good are they? If *nobody* is offering what you have to sell, don't rejoice: you may be too far ahead of a trend, or others have already failed.

Read everything you can find. There's no need to reinvent the wheel. Learn and adapt. Paula Lishman of Blackstock, Ontario, grew up in Labrador, where fur was an everyday article of clothing. Lishman studied textiles and weaving, then she invented a method of knitting strips of fur into warm, lightweight, elegant garments. While the market for traditional fur coats was in the dumps, Paula Lishman Ltd. built a business now worth $16 million a year, and opened a new market for fur in Japan, where her handknit coats sell for up to $20,000. If you can't invent, you may choose to buy the rights to a name, design, or technology; legal advice is essential if you have concerns about copyright or contracts.

Think long and hard before you enter into a business partnership, especially with your best friend. It may seem like a great idea, but friendships almost never survive the stress of building a business together, and the anger, recrimination, and guilt can destroy your company. Do you really need this person? Will she bring something to the business you cannot? Is she committed full-time, or will she disappear in a crunch?

What if your partner decides to quit? Buy you out? Sell out? If things go sour, a 50-50 partnership can lead to years of acrimony, litigation, and even the loss of your business. This said, however, wife/husband partnerships often run smoothly, and there are excellent examples of mother/daughter partnerships, where a mother brings one or more of her adult daughters into a business she has established herself. Mind you, there are wives, mothers, and daughters who would consider such partnerships perfect hell.

What about you? Ask yourself: Am I committed to this enterprise heart, soul, and body? Do I have ideas and energy to burn? Am I able to work twenty-four hours a day? Do I welcome a challenge and thrive in a crisis? Am I confident, competitive, a self-starter? Hard-headed and thick-skinned? Can I take no for an answer without feeling rejected? Can I handle fear, failure, risk, and uncertainty?

Successful entrepreneurs, women or men, are go-getters and high-fliers. The more timid among us find them aggressive, even arrogant, and they refer to themselves as workaholics, addicts, and maniacs. "We are *not* role models all women should try to emulate!" Paula Lishman warned a national conference of women entrepreneurs in November 1996. "Most people can't do it, and shouldn't try. We should come with health warnings: 'Do not try this at home unless you are sure you can handle it.'"

The courage — or foolhardiness — necessary to succeed in business is more a gut instinct than a skill to be learned. Says Lishman, "The key issue is not so much managing risk as developing an appetite for it, and an ability to digest it. The risk is what an entrepreneur eats for breakfast. It's what she slips into bed with at night. If you have no appetite for this stuff, or no ability to digest it, then get out of the game right now. You have to be able to sleep, and sleep with a clear conscience."

Risk is more than losing money. "There's a loss of self, a risk of becoming part of the business environment," says Grace White, founder and president of CanJam Trading Ltd., a Halifax import-export company with more than $13 million in annual sales. "If you work 90 to 100 hours a week, there's a loss of family time. If you have to deal with ugly people, you lose trust. I am not really interested in gaining the world and losing my soul."

Are you prepared to risk your marriage and your health? What if your family resents your frequent absences from home? Children may feel abandoned if Mum is on the phone all the time, and your anxiety level may put everyone on edge. "I was so energetic and organized I made people tired just looking at me," one business-woman confessed to me. What if your husband reacts with anger and contempt, or tries to butt in and run everything himself? Are you willing to trust your children to the care of a nanny? Are you able to handle the emotional conflict of balancing business decisions and personal relationships? Do you have a strong support network of friends and colleagues, or will you be risking loneliness and isolation?

A career with a large corporation is not necessarily good preparation. It may give women financial experience and enough capital to start a small business, but the corporate values of compliance and conformity, coupled with the security of a ritualized, hierarchical company, do not prepare women well to handle the rough-and-tumble world of private enterprise.

Risk means not knowing if, or when, you can pay yourself, or anyone else. It means working without health and pension plans, regular promotions, and paid vacations. What will happen to your company if you are in an accident or fall sick? The expenses of business ownership include extended health care and disability insurance. There is no such thing as sick leave. How much worry can you manage?

Risk also means *calculated* risk. Is it smarter to invest your money somewhere else? How objective are you about your skills and opportunities? It may be wise to buy an established company — many women do — or work for another firm to gain experience: women often spin a business off from their previous employers. Talk to people in the business — potential customers, suppliers, and clients. Listen to what they have to say, even if it's bad news, and don't be intimidated by rudeness: a nervous competitor may be trying to scare you away. If you're too shy or secretive to make a cold call, then you will have a hard time selling yourself or your product. The attitudes of the people you talk to will reveal whether you have a hot idea, or a real bummer.

Take nothing for granted. Women often think it would be nice to start a business at home so they can take care of the kids. It's murder. Cost and convenience may make it attractive, but working at home doubles the stress. Even the housework doesn't get done.

Look at the fine print. If you're renting space, is it in good condition, or will the cockroach exterminators have to come in next week? How much will it cost to fix up? Does it have a bad reputation, a history of failure? Who's out walking on the street — who makes up the foot traffic? Will they buy your products? Are there a lot of empty storefronts? Why? Is there something to build on? If there are one or two antique stores in the block, then there is room for one more, but take my advice: never locate near a high school unless you're selling pizza.

Trust your own judgment. "Don't say no to a crazy idea," says Dorothy Millman, who started a multi-million-dollar telemarketing business selling credit cards by phone from her home. Success depends on having a product or a service that catches the consumer's imagination, although at first it may be that nobody but you has ever heard of it. Your big dream may be an off-the-wall idea, or as plain as the nose on your face, a favourite hobby, or a flash of inspiration. A lot of women sell advice: they set themselves up as consultants, therapists, columnists, gardening experts, and cooking gurus. Your expertise and enthusiasm will sell your real product — yourself.

Take care, however, not to let your enthusiasm run away with you. "Keep your eye on profitability," Millman warns, "or you risk it all." You may have an excellent product, or state-of-the-art skills, but if you have no experience handling money, or phrases like "cash flow" mean nothing to you, then you'd be wise to first take courses in business management or financial planning.

Grace White, for instance, had a university degree in commerce and experience as a financial planner before she ventured into exporting fish, CanJam Trading's staple product. "I didn't even know what a mackerel was," White jokes. "I had to look it up in the encyclopedia." Similarly, Diana Joseph, founder of Calgary's Wen-Di Interiors (Chapter 14), had business experience as an accountant, but no training in interior design. Too much creative involvement can blind an entrepreneur to the hard reality of the bottom line.

This is where a "business plan" comes in. You don't *have* to have a business plan unless you need a bank loan, but Jerry White's study showed that 90 percent of successful businesswomen have a plan prepared by a *professional adviser*. The purpose of the plan is to enable you to explain your scheme to others, and to force you to think it through yourself. An investment of $1,000 at this stage can save you $1 million later.

The basic components of a plan are these:

- a description of the business
- an estimate of start-up costs, return on investment, market position
- a detailed marketing plan
- details of operation, including staff and suppliers
- company structure
- financial data

The plan will determine whether you will have enough money coming in to pay your bills when they come due. It takes time to build a customer base. Err on the side of caution: assume it will cost twice as much, and take twice as long to collect. On the other hand, if you hit a roll and your company takes off, don't be crippled by a hidebound, irrelevant business plan. Go with the flow. Innovate, adapt, expand, and plan as you go.

Start small, but don't undervalue your product. "Look over the horizon," advises Paula Lishman. "Don't dream too small." Lishman was warned that the Japanese market was impossible to crack; today, she sells 70 percent of her fur garments to Japan. Your selling price may be expensive or economical, but the key to your success is profit margin: how much did it cost you to produce? A writer, for instance, may sell a magazine article for $4,000. If the story takes two days to write, that's good money, but if it takes two months, this writer is in financial trouble.

Selling products and services that appeal to an upscale, high-end consumer, or a captive market, is a better risk than trying to compete with a mass-market retailer like Zellers. Remember, a $15-million business is still a small business, and most women are in small business. Customers will seek out a small business because it offers quality, service, and something they can't find anywhere else.

That "something" is often the owner herself. New clients like to deal with "the boss," and a good boss will be on the phone to customers, or on the shop floor, long after her business has expanded to include receptionists, managers, and hundreds of employees. Schmoozing, charming, soothing, convincing, and *selling* are the key to success in any business, and don't be shocked if you also sweep the floor and wash the windows.

Forget the babe-in-the-blue-pinstripe-suit stereotype of the businesswoman. The boss may be wearing blue jeans or sweatpants, and, like Eva House (Chapter 13), she may be bald. Good businesswomen dress for themselves and their clientele. If you are working primarily on the phone, why blow $10,000 on suits and shoes? But if you're not Joni Mitchell, should you wear a flower-power dress to a corporate board meeting?

The boss can't do everything, although some women accept this reality reluctantly. Many people, like me, are perfectly happy with a one-woman show, but most business owners need employees. "Nothing can promote growth like a good hire early on," says Lishman. "Hire carefully, hire well, cultivate relationships. Prune rot before it spreads."

This is good advice, and often ignored. As a customer in women-owned shops, I often encounter salespeople who natter to friends on the phone, squabble among themselves, trash the boss, and treat me as if I were a bag lady. Who hired these creeps? Poorly paid part-time workers can cause more trouble than they're worth, and an inexperienced boss can easily be manipulated by her employees into doing what *they* want. She may assume that their hissy fits and sullen resistance are all *her* fault. What is she doing wrong? How can she appease them? She can't, of course. Instead, she feels guilty, resentful, and depressed. Her business suffers.

Let's get rid of the stereotype that women are, by nature, compassionate, nurturing, and consensus-seeking. Phooey. No business-woman is obliged to treat her staff as friends, family, or partners. She is not Brown Owl. Firing irritating or incompetent people is one of the most painful, but necessary, lessons a businesswoman has to learn.

Trouble can be avoided, however, by training your own people, paying them what they're worth and giving them responsibility. Incentives such as bonuses, promotions, and shares in the company encourage productivity; weak performers will eliminate themselves. Giving responsibility, however, includes sharing company information, even when that information is sensitive or embarrassing.

"When I wasn't profitable for the first time, I didn't tell anybody," confesses Toronto fashion designer Linda Lundström (Chapter 12). "The pressure of having to deal with the bad news by myself almost killed me." Lundström adopted a policy of transparency: she communicates with everyone in the company, right down to the sewing machine operators. It's been a boost for morale: "People love information," she says. "They can't get enough." In turn, her employees give her feedback at regular meetings Lundström calls her "whine and cheese" parties.

Since women entrepreneurs are new at the game, they are receptive to innovation. For instance, it's often possible to transfer responsibility from employees to self-employed contractors. Susan Bradley, who founded the SumBunny's line of children's clothing in her Brantford, Ontario, home in 1990, markets her clothing primarily through a national network of sales reps who buy her clothes wholesale and sell them at house parties. Bradley is relieved of responsibility for their salaries and the cost of retail outlets, and the saleswomen become entrepreneurs themselves.

A successful entrepreneur recognizes her weaknesses and hires someone who can provide those missing skills. Dorothy Millman says, "Ask yourself, 'What am I really good at? Would I pay me to do what I am doing? Can I find someone to do it at a cheaper rate?'" Don't waste your time counting toothpicks or licking stamps. A successful businesswoman will usually have a strong, silent cadre of managers, team leaders, partners, and investors who have shared in her company's growth for many years. One of them might be her husband.

One of them is not likely to be her bank manager. Bank managers, men or women, continue to be the Big, Bad Wolves stalking women entrepreneurs. We have no banks owned by women, full of women's money, with women presidents anxious to lend money to women entrepreneurs. Success makes no difference. You can have $1 million in your savings account, and your bank manager will phone you at 5 p.m. on the Friday before Christmas to call your loan. "They'll ask you to mortgage your house, your cottage, and your children's education, then they'll ask for your husband's statement of net worth," says Beverley Topping, president of Today's Parent Group.

A bank won't consider a loan without a business plan, but your manager might not even glance at it. "Banks will make a snap judgement," says Topping. "If the chemistry is right, you'll go to second base. There's nothing you can do to manufacture chemistry. In 75 percent of the cases, I *knew* I wasn't going to do business with these guys."

Although the Canadian banks are promoting programs designed to encourage women entrepreneurs, at the branch level women still face ignorance, misunderstanding, and discrimination. I recently spoke to a bookstore owner who's been in business twenty years. "It's not getting any better," she sighed. "It's not because we're women, I think, but because we're *small.*" Carol Denman, president of Atchison & Denman Court Reporting (Chapter 10), laughs: "If I had to do it all over again, I'd start my own little bank for all us 'little ladies' with our 'little businesses.'"

How to get big? This is the next challenge, and to meet it women will need to tap into the deep wells of capital that have traditionally been available to men. In today's mercurial, unpredictable economy, businesses that fail to grow and change will stagnate and die. Taking care of business means having your feet firmly on the ground, and your eyes on the future.

RELISHING TASTE AND TRADITION

MARY KELEKIS

By Helen Stein

KELEKIS RESTAURANT

By Larry Geller, a former Winnipeg North Ender, September 1977
Canadian Dimensions

The place of tall, Greek women.
The place through which a part
Of every evening flowed.

Lawyer tables and bowling shirts ...
Memories of Antiochus fade ...
The hellenizers pick up Yiddish intonations.
The isle of Lemnos and Aegean nights,
Gleam in a woman's hair.

Fame is a wall of pictures
Where actor and politician
Jostle for the eye.
"We all have eaten here," they say ...

Or of a summer moontide,
Stood outside the order-window
Shuffling barefoot on a sidewalk
Richly decked in sunflower shells.
Stood looking in on steaming cookers
Waiting for dispensation of hot potato chips
In fragrant bags of brown

Papa Kelekis, rich in years and daughters,
Raised his monumental name
Beside the river of flowing cars.

The years run fast,
And every night, men with greying hair,
And older women come in trances ...
Looking for their youth

"1946. I lived on Stella, I had brown hair then."
"My father delivered bread
He used to bring me Saturday mornings."
"We were engaged at Kelekis ...
My grandson comes now every weekend."

Well you couldn't just go home
After the movie
An evening, like a speech, demands
a decisive conclusion.

We sat and wove the terminal hours ...
We sat and savoured the grey
In the braiding tresses of the decades ...
We noted the departures ...
The names migrating to California,
To Toronto, gone west,
Or chiselled into stone
In sleeping parks.

We bring our babies,
For the Greek sisters to admire,
Submissive to traditions
We scarcely understand.

A place for encores and aftermaths.
A place, when Cuban Missile Crisis came,
To have chips and a Coke.

And if I have the time,
The night before the Armageddon War,
I'll go down to Kelekis.

As guest of honour at the 1996 Wish and Chips Charity Dinner in Winnipeg, Mary Kelekis received warm congratulations on the success of her business from representatives of three levels of government — Winnipeg's mayor, Susan Thompson; premier of Manitoba Gary filmon; and minister of foreign affairs Lloyd Axworthy — all satisfied customers.

The event, sponsored by the Manitoba Restaurant and Foodservices Association in support of the Children's Wish Foundation, marked C. Kelekis Restaurant's fiftieth year at 1100 Main Street in Winnipeg. The business itself has operated since 1931, when Mary's father, a Greek immigrant, started selling french fries from a converted Model T truck. Kelekis, the oldest restaurant in Manitoba run by original owners, holds a special place in the hearts of its patrons.

Mayor Thompson said, "I am proud to share in this occasion as the Kelekis family name is synonymous with business leadership, generosity, and, of course, great food."

Premier Filmon sent a videotaped message in which he recalled, "Growing up in the North End, I spent many an afternoon and many an allowance in Kelekis enjoying one of their famous hot-dog-and-fries plates. I and thousands of loyal customers continue to enjoy Kelekis's great food and unique atmosphere. It is a North

End institution that is now virtually a part of Manitoba's cultural identity."

In a letter from Ottawa, Axworthy wrote, "A lot of things have changed in Winnipeg since the days I grew up in the North End. I'm glad that C. Kelekis Restaurant is not one of them. More than just a spot for good food, it is a gathering place, a meeting place, a place for friends and family. In my own version of 'wish and chips,' it has been a place where more than a few political dreams and strategies have been discussed over a plate of those famous fries."

Clearly, nostalgia is one ingredient in the restaurant's longevity. "Some people come straight from the airport, to make sure we're still here," Mary says, laughing. But you don't have to have lived in Winnipeg to be a fan. Cookbook author Bonnie Stern travelled from Toronto in 1978 to research an article for *Canadian Living*, in which she concluded, after tasting Kelekis's hot dogs and french fries, that they qualified as "gourmet food." She recently chose Kelekis as one of her ten favourite "food finds" across Canada. Stern says, "I was looking for places that reflect a sense of love or of community — and, of course, the food's delicious."

To check it out for myself, I drive to Winnipeg's historic Portage and Main corner and head north down Main Street past the Winnipeg Centennial Concert Hall, the Manitoba Museum, City Hall, then the seedy hotels, pawn shops, and the Mission House Soup Kitchen. Fourteen blocks farther down Main Street, across from the grey rectangular buildings of the Holy Family Nursing Home, the orange and blue C. Kelekis Restaurant sign appears above a red-brick-faced building, which is dwarfed by the Shopper's Drug Mart next to it. The aroma of french fries wafts invitingly through the parking lot adjacent to the restaurant. Inside, between two U-shaped lunch counters, there are deep fryers and a large grill sizzling with wieners and burgers. Sunlight streams through the large picture window, while people seated on orange vinyl swivel chairs watch the staff prepare their orders. "My father always wanted the customers to be able to see us cooking the food," says Mary.

She's about to leave the lunch area and enter the dining room when a man standing near the front of the restaurant calls out to her, "Not before you give me a hug." She turns around for a warm embrace over the take-out counter. Later, Mary tells me the man is Doug Stephen, past president of both the provincial and national restaurant associations. I ask her about the hug. "The guys like me," she explains, shrugging her shoulders. "And I have the greatest respect for my fellow restaurateurs."

Beyond the counter area, the dining room is windowless and illuminated by four massive lantern-style chandeliers that cast a golden warmth. A grey-haired man silently leads me to one of the woodgrain Arborite-topped tables, barely pausing to indicate that this is my stop. A waiter in black pants and a red shirt sets down a paper place mat, menu, an order form — and a yellow pencil. He leaves without introducing himself or telling me he'll be my waiter today. This is one place where they don't waste time stating the obvious. But the service is deft and professional, and the absence of pretension could well be another factor in the restaurant's success.

The menu offers a good selection of sandwiches, salads, hot dogs, and hamburgers, along with several dinner items. The most expensive meals are the veal cutlet and pork chop dinners — both are priced at $8.95 and include roll and butter, cole slaw, and french fries or mashed potatoes. I order fish and chips at $6.95. As I finish the plate of lightly battered halibut, the best cole slaw I've tasted, and those famous fries — thin, crisp on the outside and tender inside — I make a mental note to do more field work on this project. (On my next visit, I research the hot dog, which also lives up to its reputation. And the Greek salad, although not as renowned as the specialties, is generously topped with creamy feta cheese and calamata olives.) Mary tells me the hot dogs are made with wieners that come from the supplier with only one special attribute — their eight-inch length — and that they are deep-fried before they hit the grill. The french fries, which once sold at five cents for a small bag, now cost $1.25 for a regular order and $1.50

for a large. A possible key to their quality is that they are blanched in hot oil, then deep-fried when they're ordered. They're made with Manitoba potatoes, and not just any Manitoba potatoes. A supplier told me Mary once insisted that a whole delivery (from another wholesaler) be loaded up and returned because they were the wrong kind of potatoes.

The waiter and his female counterpart, also wearing dark pants and a red shirt, file briskly back and forth carrying trays of hot dogs and fries, hamburgers and fries, and fish and fries. The restaurant can seat eighty, and at 1:30 on a Saturday afternoon it is filled with young couples with and without children, middle-aged men and women with and without elderly parents, and a few singles. Towards the back of the room a television set flickers on an overhead shelf. Beyond that is a utility area for staff, with coffee pots, drink dispensers, and a sink above which is a hand-printed reminder: "WASH YOUR HANDS." Centred high on the back wall is a large banner proclaiming "C. KELEKIS — Celebrating 60 Years." Mary says it should be updated to 65. Behind the pass-through where the waiters pick up their orders, two white-uniformed cooks perform their duties with solemn efficiency. Suinn Anderson has worked in the Kelekis kitchen for twenty-eight years, Anne Zentner for seventeen. Anderson says neither the menu nor people's tastes in food have changed much during her time on staff. When I ask Mary why they don't serve more Greek food, she replies, "Well, because it's not a Greek restaurant."

From time to time, Mary leaves the cash register to walk her rounds, talking with customers and making sure everything is as it should be — neither activity does she take lightly. In fact, there's very little Mary takes lightly. Whether it's in the restaurant, or in the community where her leadership and volunteer work have earned her shopping bags full of commendations, Mary admits she likes to "make sure everyone's doing what they're supposed to be doing." It's a trait some people appreciate more than others. She works seven days a week, arriving before 8 a.m. to open up, and seldom getting home before nine in the evening — except on weekends, when she works a longer shift. Mary is seventy-two years old.

"I love what I'm doing," she explains. "Meeting up with people is the most fascinating thing — just absolutely wonderful. Life is an adventure, but you've got to be out there or you'll miss it. Why, just last week, on Valentine's Day, a young couple came in the restaurant and he got down on his knees and proposed to the young lady. She said yes," Mary recalls with genuine delight. "There was a bit of a squeal and all excitement. He gave her the ring and she was rushing to the phone, I guess to tell her folks. So I went up to them and gave her some carnations from one of the tables and congratulated them. And we decided, heck, it's a big day for them and we picked up the bill for their dinner."

Mary's dark hair has turned grey and she pushes her solid, five-foot-five frame forward at a different pace than when she could run faster and jump higher than anyone else at Daniel McIntyre High School. She's dressed in tailored grey pants and a mustard-yellow thick cotton shirt that complements her smooth olive-toned skin. She wears no jewellery except a ring with a large turquoise stone on her left pinky finger and a wide gold band on the same finger of her right hand. Everything about her, from her well-cut short hair to her sensible black leather shoes, reflects the understated excellence and authenticity that characterize the restaurant.

Mary says it's her sisters who are a bit slower and older now; Chryse, eighty-two, and Evelyn, seventy-seven, work the evening shift. But she concedes she usually drives home in the afternoon for a half-hour nap before coming back, "rejuvenated and feeling great," to help take care of the dinner crowd. She and her three surviving sisters own the business jointly. Becky, the youngest (who runs a travel agency with her husband), looks after the restaurant's accounting. Mary has worked in the family business full-time since 1944. For many years, she and her sisters did everything in the restaurant, including the cooking and cleaning. "My father was very upset the first time we tried to hire a cook," says Mary, who shared the role of general manager with her sister Sophie until 1980. With the deaths of her parents, a brother, and two sisters over the years, Mary feels not only sadness at the loss of members of a loving family, but also the burden of heading the business without them. (Sophie died in 1980, Leo in 1993, and Isobel in 1996.)

But Mary does understand the operation inside and out. And, although she employs twenty people, she knows how to do everything that needs to be done, how to diagnose every equipment problem, and who to call for the few she can't fix herself. She also knows what it takes to exceed customers' expectations and how to keep staff happy enough that they stay for decades. But even Mary can't fully explain the Kelekis phenomenon.

From the Wall of Fame on the north side of the dining room, photographs of Pierre Trudeau, Harry Belafonte, Al Waxman, Monty Hall, and dozens of other celebrities smile above the diners. Hockey legend Bobby Hull signed his photo: "To the greatest folks in town with the greatest food in the world." Others bear similar sentiments.

"When Trudeau came, the last time he campaigned in the seventies, they sent the RCMP six weeks before he arrived, to check out the restaurant," Mary recalls. "They wanted to make sure it was safe for the prime minister. Apparently it was okay, and they said to expect the prime minister on such and such a day. Well, when he came here, his security had stationed someone at our back door and closed off the street so no cars could come into the parking lot. When the prime minister and his party arrived — they came on a double-decker bus — there were eight or ten people in the restaurant and they weren't allowed to leave. The front and back doors were locked. The prime minister had a hot dog and met all my sisters and my family. We talked and had some pictures taken."

Mary is at the restaurant every day of the week because she feels responsible for making sure everything is up to her standards. But she's there for another reason, too. "I'd be lost if I didn't come in," she says, admitting that the three days the restaurant was closed for Christmas made her a little antsy. "I got to sleep in three mornings in a row, but then I didn't know what to do with myself. You look forward to seeing the people you work with, your staff. They're good people and I care what's happening with them. And the customers you haven't seen for a long time — you just never know when they're going to show up, and I'm always worried I'm going to miss something."

She's glad she didn't miss Tony award–winning actor Len Cariou when he dropped in during the Christmas season. "And the fellow we named our Yaleburger after. He was just here from his home in the Caribbean," she says, explaining that as an adolescent this customer would come from his grandfather's house, nearby, and always ask for tomato, lettuce, and mayo on his cheeseburger. "So we finally named it after him. It's still on the menu, and he's a dear friend."

Another of those longtime friends who comes back to visit is Monty Hall. Long before he hosted the popular game show "Let's Make a Deal," Hall made deliveries, by bicycle every Saturday, from his father's North End butcher shop. In a videotaped greeting he sent to the Wish and Chips dinner from his home in Los Angeles, he recalls how his first stop was always Kelekis for a bag of "chips" to sustain him while he pedalled through town with 100 pounds of meat in his carrier.

"It's not just running a restaurant," says Mary, "it's being friends with your customers. It's a personal connection, very personal. They're not just customers; they're friends."

But there are those who find Mary more contrary. One Winnipegger, who chooses to remain anonymous, recalls taking a family gathering of fifteen to the restaurant in 1993. Everything was fine until two latecomers, visitors from Toronto, arrived to join the group. To accommodate them, the family borrowed a couple of chairs from a nearby table, placing them at the end of the area where their group was seated. That's when, according to the customer, Mary swooped down on them, shouting that they were blocking a fire exit. The Torontonians left in shock, and the host (a former Kelekis regular) claims he's still mad at Mary. "We never go back there," he rages. "Except when the kids are in town and they insist," he adds sheepishly.

Albert Sumka, president of Sumka Bros. Wholesale Vegetables Ltd., which has supplied Kelekis with potatoes since the fifties, says it's true that Mary can get madder than a hornet. "If something isn't right, she'll let you know about it," he chuckles. "She tells me off, but it's just part of doing business. She's a good person, though, and honest."

Kelekis gives new meaning to the term "take-out." Mary says, "I had a lady in here two weeks ago, took eighteen hot dogs back to California, all ready to eat. What she does is she puts them in her microwave when she gets home, and they're just like off the grill. There's also one young lady whose sisters moved to Calgary. She misses them and when she goes to visit, well, you've never seen so much food going outa here, going to Calgary — I parcel up the whole works for her — hot dogs, cheeseburgers, and fries."

Then there's the couple who flew Mary — and enough wieners and hamburger patties to feed eighty guests — to Toronto for their pre-wedding supper. "I sent the food on a Thursday night by Air Canada," Mary recalls. "Someone picked it up at the airport, and the next day I flew out. I went into the kitchen and supervised what they were doing and how they were doing it."

She has even served up her famous fries and hot dogs at the Winnipeg Centennial Concert Hall, and although she can't remember the year, she believes the occasion was a disco party. And in June 1985, 2,000 people jammed the restaurant and spilled out into the parking lot as they gathered in Winnipeg to celebrate St. John's Technical High School's seventy-fifth anniversary. A couple of years before, it was a similar scene, but then they were there to celebrate the Kelekis business's fiftieth.

On the wall opposite the celebrity photos, a hand-painted mural by local artist John Tutura depicts the history of the Kelekis dynasty. Tutura, whose murals appear in several Winnipeg buildings, is a former North Ender who remembers his grandmother taking him to Kelekis for those five-cent bags of chips. The mural tells part of the Kelekis story — how Chrys Kelekis emigrated from Turkey in 1913, following his beloved Magdalene Maria, who was brought to Canada by her older brother after the death of her parents. Chrys and Magdalene married in Montreal and had their first two children — Chryse and Fotina. "It was during the First World War," says Mary, "and my father ended up being foreman, if you please, in a munitions factory with a whole bunch of Italians. I don't know how my dad conquered the English language, but he managed." After two years, the young couple moved to Edmonton, where Sophie was born in 1918, and then to Winnipeg, where Chrys found the air better for his asthma. He sold peanuts and popcorn from a pushcart to make a living for his growing family, and he and Magdalene continued to make baby girls — seven in all. This did not impress Chrys's father, back in Turkey. "My grandfather was very upset with my father for leaving him," says Mary. "He didn't forgive him until 1928, when my brother was born after all these girls."

By this time, Chrys had ventured into the confectionery business. "He was a real entrepreneur, out there trying to figure out what to do for a living," says Mary. But the death of his daughter Fotina from pneumonia at the age of fourteen, marked the beginning of a series of misfortunes. The family had been living above the confectionery store, when it was destroyed by fire. "After everyone else was out of the building, my father had just carried me down the stairs when they collapsed behind him," says Mary, who was a baby at the time. "So he really was my guardian angel."

Chrys tried again, but lost his second confectionery shop when a partner ran off without paying his share of the bills. "Those were hard years in the thirties," Mary recalls. "There were very few Greek people in Winnipeg to help him do anything, so whatever he did, he had to struggle on his own and work it out. We had to go on what was called relief at the time, until my dad came up with the idea to sell peanuts and popcorn from a truck. He had made a lot of friends when he was in the confectionery business, and I believe they helped him put this idea into reality. Dad wasn't afraid to try anything."

Although others have said Mr. Kelekis was a tough taskmaster with his daughters, I notice that Mary, who is purportedly pretty tough herself, gets tears in her eyes whenever I ask her to talk about her father — forty years after his death. "My parents were crazy about one another, and we used to have such fun times with my dad," she recalls, her dark brown eyes filling. "We'd go to hockey games with him, football games, he was a fun guy to be with. And he loved his sports. When we had the truck at hockey games, he'd spend most of the time in the rink while we looked after the customers. He'd come out between periods to see how we were doing. My mother was happy just to see that he was happy. She never worked in the restaurant, but kept things going for him at home."

Mary remembers her mother as "a real trouper" — hard-working, a diabetic who, when she had to have a leg amputated, joked to horrified friends, "Look, they cut my leg off, but I'm not worried because I have good sons-in-law to take care of me." Magdalene lived to the age of seventy-four and, besides being a helpmate to her husband, instilled her Greek Orthodox faith in her children.

Looking at the mural, Mary smiles as she describes how all the Kelekis children helped in the business, but considered it fun and exciting. "When my father found this was a way he could count on to make a living for his family, he wanted his daughters involved. And every one of us was. When you think about women working and looking after something like this, you know, it's quite a task. They talk about women's libbers the last number of years. Well, he had us liberated years ago. We were out there working with people and looking after a business. Women today, all of a sudden they're doing that, but we were doing it then. We had to work alongside Dad, we had to make sure the orders were in and that we got our supplies. Well, after all, he couldn't do everything, so he gave us the responsibility to go ahead and do it. And that's what made it so interesting. He always told us: 'You gotta think; you gotta work; you gotta know what's going on. You have to go forward.'" She recalls that when he opened his first take-out restaurant in 1944, they were all putting in eighteen hours a day. "Those were the best times," she says, "when we were younger."

One of Mary's first memories of helping in the family business is when truckloads of potatoes were delivered to the Kelekis home. "I'd think nothing of carrying a sack of potatoes across the basement and stacking them in the corner," she says. As youngsters, Mary and her sisters peeled up to 500 pounds of potatoes daily and made a game of it. "We'd see who could do it the fastest," she says. She remembers carrying pails of cut-up potatoes on the streetcar to wherever her father had his customized truck parked. Now, in the restaurant's immaculate basement, a machine the size of a hot-water tank peels fifty pounds in a minute. A smaller gizmo cuts them into fries in forty-five seconds.

When Chrys Kelekis died in 1957 at the age of sixty-eight, the family faced some tough decisions. The liquor licence Chrys had applied for arrived the day after his death. His daughters chose not to keep it, for two reasons: it might invite trouble for a business run by women, and it would change the nature of the restaurant. "We didn't need that," says Mary. "People bring their children here." They also closed a snack shop that Papa Kelekis had opened nearby in 1944, and focused their energy on the restaurant at 1100 Main Street; it had been built there in 1946, expanded in 1955, and was completely renovated in 1977.

To succeed, Mary believes, you have to have confidence in yourself and your product. You have to love what you're doing, and you have to care about your customers. "People came to my dad's restaurant for the food, but also because they liked to talk to him. Eventually they'd marry and we'd see them with their first child, and the next thing you know it's their grandchildren coming in. To stay in business, you have to give something good to people so they'll want to come back. My sisters and I have always been very particular, making sure everything is spotless and just so."

About finances, Mary will say only the business is holding its own. But with customers consuming 60,000 to 80,000 hot dogs annually, not to mention the mountains of fries and other food, this might be a modest assessment. "I know of some people who start doing well," she says, "but instead of putting money back into the business, they're living high off the hog, and then their business suffers. They'll decide they need a better car, a bigger house, but you have to remember you have bills to pay, your people to look after — make sure all these things are taken care of before you go out and buy luxuries."

As in most restaurants, employees start at minimum wage, and Mary defends the industry's resistance to increasing that amount. "This is the first job for a lot of people, and you're going to turn around and give them a big wage! We train these people, and they go out in the world better for it," she says, adding that her long-term employees are well-paid. Mary says she can be a softy with her staff but that she also lays down the law. "If they're not pulling their share of the load, I let them know. I have to, and they understand that I'm concerned about my business being run in a proper way," she says. "I get after the young ones, 'Why are you dressing that way — you're not coming in here dressing like that — funky dressing and stuff like that, it's not right.'"

But she also listens to their troubles, and over the years the sisters have convinced some young people to stay in school and out of trouble. "I had one little girl working for us who had left home and wasn't talking to her parents," Mary recalls. "I told her: 'That's foolish, don't do that. If you want to leave home, tell your parents. But don't lose touch with them.' They were on the outs for a little while, but now everything's fine."

When McGavin Food Ltd. featured Mary as customer of the month in August 1994, they thanked her for being such a loyal customer and said they looked forward to another sixty-three years of supplying the restaurant with bread and buns. Winnipeg Old Country Sausage Ltd., which had always supplied the famous Kelekis wieners, was shut down by fire in October 1996. Mary found another supplier, but made it clear from the start that the arrangement would be temporary. So, when Winnipeg Old Country reopened its doors three months later, they knew they could count on orders from Kelekis. "But I don't see sales people after 11 a.m.

any more. They have to come and see me in the morning — unless they have a flat tire," she says, adding that they're all very good about fitting into her schedule.

Chrys Kelekis's only son, Leo, a lawyer, was president of the family company until his death in 1993 at the age of sixty-five. He and Mary, the only two siblings who didn't marry, shared the family home. Leo, who was becoming an excellent cook in his spare time, would call Mary when he got home from his law office to see when she'd be leaving work. When she arrived, he'd have dinner ready. Now, younger sister Becky, who lives just across the street from Mary, on Wellington Crescent (one of Winnipeg's older upscale neighbourhoods), has her over for dinner often. "She understands my situation," Mary says softly.

Mary sometimes asks sisters Chryse and Evelyn to come to work early so she can attend a game of hockey or football, usually with her nephew's children. "I love spending time with the kids," she says. In 1968 Mary served as the first female president of the YMCA in western Canada. ("I just went there to learn to swim," she says.) She was elected president of the Manitoba Restaurant and Foodservices Association in 1987 — again, the first woman to hold that position. And in 1990 she was inducted into the Folk Arts Hall of Fame for her work in helping establish Winnipeg's annual festival of nations — Folklorama — a major multicultural event since 1970. "They had a special 'Founder' badge made for me, so people wouldn't question what I'm doing when I go around checking up on things," she says. "It's immaterial whether I should or shouldn't, but I care about it and I want it to be a success. That's all there is to it."

The courage and determination a young Greek couple brought to Canada early in this century keep showing up in their offspring. A few years ago, as Mary's two older sisters closed the restaurant after 1 a.m. and approached their car, two men with a gun demanded that one sister give them her coat. She refused and stood her ground until a witness shouted that he had called the police. Mary says, "The men grabbed my sister's handbag and ran like hell." Now Mary faces another challenge, having to work double shifts while Evelyn is needed at home with her seriously ill husband. "We've always had a Kelekis in charge whenever the restaurant is open, so I'm not sure what I'm going to do," says Mary. But she has no plans to retire and is incensed by the rumours that surface periodically, usually after the death of a family member, about the establishment being up for sale. "We have never, ever, ever tried to sell," she says defiantly. "This is ours. We watched the basement being poured, the walls going up. My sisters and I have worked too hard and put too much into it to give it up.

"We know that eventually we won't be able to be working any more," she concedes. "But as long as we are able, we will continue."

Life is still an adventure — and Mary's not about to miss it.

2   LIGHTING THE WAY
JULIA LEVY

By Diana Luckow

Serendipity isn't a word you'd expect to hear tripping from a scientist's tongue but it's a word that Dr. Julia Levy, president, chief executive officer, and chief scientific officer of QLT PhotoTherapeutics Inc., uses quite frequently when telling her business story. Serendipity, that mysterious faculty of finding valuable or agreeable things not sought for, seems to be something that Levy encounters, often, although no one would dispute how incredibly hard she has worked to achieve her goals.

An eminent Vancouver immunologist and microbiology professor, Levy has spent much of the last sixteen years mixing science with business in order to commercialize research that began in her laboratory at the University of British Columbia almost twenty years ago. Today, she's as comfortable in the boardroom as she is at the lab bench and, remarkably, very successful in both environments.

QLT, the biotechnology company she co-founded sixteen years ago, is now British Columbia's largest, with a market value of $820 million, which ranks it fourth among Canada's biotechnology health-care companies. It is also the first B.C. biotech company to bring its product, a light-activated drug called PHOTOFRIN, to market, and one of only three in Canada to do so. "They're seen as our premier biotech company," says Susan Kingsley of Kingsley and Associates, a management and communications consultant to the biopharmaceutical industry in British Columbia. "They've done it."

Today, in QLT's offices overlooking the Cambie Street bridge in Vancouver, sixty-two-year-old Levy, dressed down for "casual Friday" in pale green jeans, matching sweatshirt, and mock hiking boots, takes an hour out from her usual fourteen-hour business day to talk about how she did it. Her half-grown Rottweiler pup Lucy, which she walked to work from her condo on Granville Island, is busy gnawing on lava rocks dug up from around a plant in a corner of the boardroom.

Elsewhere in the building, 115 employees are at work in quality-control labs, research labs, or offices, toiling over the company's business — the research and development of light-activated drugs, a biomedical field called photodynamic therapy that Levy pioneered and for which she has high hopes. "It's a wonderful treatment for early cancers," she says. "It's very benign, it's a wonderful technology."

Levy began exploring photodynamic therapy in the seventies, working with light-activated drugs and disease-fighting antibodies. It was in 1978 that she first recognized her research could have commercial potential for the treatment of cancer. She'd found a way to hitch a drug molecule to an antibody and create a "magic bullet" that could target cancer cells and, when the drug was exposed to light, destroy the cells. She reasoned that this type of light-sensitive, or photodynamic, therapy could be a boon to cancer patients since, without exposure to light, the drugs weren't harmful.

In retrospect, the research was the easy part. Finding a way to bring her product to market in Canada was incredibly difficult since she was pioneering a technology in an industry that was non-existent in British Columbia and only just beginning in eastern Canada. Still, Levy was determined to commercialize her research and to do it in Canada.

Levy's determination and motivation stem from her ambition to make a difference in the world, a goal she's been chasing since her teens, although she can't explain where this need comes from. Creating a better way to treat cancer, a disease that has terrified her since she first learned about it when studying microbiology at UBC in the mid-fifties, is one way to make that difference.

Levy still remembers when she became fascinated by how cells can become so aberrant and, at the same time, can be so obedient. "I remember becoming totally awed that, billions of times to one, everything works right and that we're not all a mess of patients," she recalls. "That's a moment of truth that I still remember. That led to an interest in what was going on when cells didn't behave themselves properly."

Although her parents didn't comprehend her burning desire to become a scientist, Levy persevered. She graduated from Magee High School at age fifteen (she'd skipped Grades 2 and 4) and then lied about her age and her ability to type in order to land a job at B.C. Hydro's gas and distribution division, where she worked for a year to earn money for university. At the same time, she took first-year university at night school, then attended day classes at UBC for the next three years. In 1955, she graduated with an honours B.A. in microbiology and immunology.

Later that year, with new husband Howard Gerwing in tow, she headed for London, England, where her husband, a history graduate, did research in the Hudson's Bay Archives while she earned a Ph.D. in microbiology in 1958. She was just twenty-three years old when she returned to UBC as a professor of microbiology, a position she still holds today, although she no longer teaches. "I was in a hurry," she laughs now. "I don't know why, but I was."

She still is in a hurry — to experience life, say her colleagues and associates. "She's the type of person who wants to do as much as possible in life, whether it's business or outside activities," says QLT's senior vice-president and chief financial officer, Ken Galbraith. He now accompanies her on road trips and says, "I'm thirty-four and Julia's sixty-four and it amazes me that we can travel on long trips, work twelve to fourteen hours a day and she always seems more refreshed than I am."

"Julia Levy is a woman of almost unlimited energy and great dedication," says Max Cairns, vice-president of the Science Council of British Columbia, who worked extensively with her during the early years of QLT's start-up. "She has incredible stamina; the amount and range of things she tackles is phenomenal."

"I have a huge energy drive to finish things, to complete what I start," admits Levy. "That's part of my thrill." In fact, she says, she can become obsessive about finishing tasks, even if it's just finishing a report or clearing her desk. "I like reaching milestones, that's what I've always lived by."

Commercializing her research at first appeared to be a milestone Levy wouldn't manage, but she was saved when four colleagues who were also interested in starting a research and development company asked her to join them. In 1981, they founded Quadra Logic Technologies Inc., a name they later changed to QLT Photo-Therapeutics Inc.

Going into partnership, says Levy, was exciting. "It was like broadening the collaboration, it was like new frontiers. We were all walking into a strange environment and waiting to see how it all shook down." She took on the mantle of chief scientific officer and vice-president, a position she held until February 1995, when she became president and CEO.

"All of us were incredibly naïve," she says now. "What none of us understood when we got into this was the incredible complexity of drug development." Sure, they'd heard that it could take ten years and $100 to $200 million to bring lab research to market, but none of them believed it. Today, $150 million later, Levy believes. "It really is true," she says, "which is horrifying — it just seems like it shouldn't have to cost that much to get a drug into the marketplace."

The high cost of biotechnology ultimately led Levy and her partners to form strategic partnerships in order to grow their company, a strategy that has mostly worked well and that QLT continues to foster.

In the beginning, however, the partners funded their business with research grants. When those weren't enough, they upped the ante, each investing $50,000. To raise her share, Levy borrowed the money. The partners also did a private share offering, luring $300,000 out of their colleagues' pockets.

"Our first investors did very well, thank God," says Levy. "They were long on faith and probably not too high on the knowledge of how amateurish we were at that point." She recalls a particularly nightmarish project where they tried to sell antibody-based pregnancy kits to China. "It was a naïve attempt to generate revenues in the short term," comments Levy now. "We found out quickly enough that Chinese businessmen weren't lining up with their chequebooks open. What they really wanted to do was barter condoms, which all failed to blow up when they were tested." She still cringes at the memory.

They made a lot of mistakes in the early days. Since they were each pursuing their own research projects, there was no product or market focus; they supported anything that looked capable of initiating funding or partnerships. The ill-fated antibody-pregnancy kit is one example; another was a diagnostic lung cancer test for which Levy was awarded a gold medal from the Science Council of British Columbia, but which, during clinical testing, turned out not to have a high enough level of specificity and sensitivity to be marketable. Difficulties like this, however, are just part of science, she says. "Only about 10 percent of things that look promising are successful at the end of clinical testing."

By 1985 Levy's photodynamic research into second-generation photosensitive drugs began to look like their most promising business option; the partners agreed to focus a business plan around it. "It was a niche that we could attain a leadership in," she says. "So much of the other stuff was highly competitive; we knew we could get eaten for lunch by a big company that was incredibly competitive."

Still, once the others' research was sidelined, they began to lose interest. Of the five partners, only Jim Miller, a physiology professor, and Levy went the distance. Miller's entrepreneurial instincts and vision complemented Levy's scientific prowess. Together, says Levy, they made a dynamite combination. "Our product was science," she says. "I made the product, he did the marketing. He and I worked together so well, like yin and yang. I don't think QLT would have ever happened if he and I hadn't been there together."

Miller, who left QLT in 1991 to develop another biotech company, Inex Pharmaceuticals Corp., isn't quite so pessimistic. "I imagine QLT may not have been the same as it is today in terms of where it's going and what it's doing," he says. He attributes the success of the firm to the combination of Levy's scientific skills and the strong team of competent business management people within the organization. "The science has certainly pushed it," he says, "but if the business skills hadn't been in the company, the company wouldn't be what it is today."

The pair proved to have a knack for raising financing, something that doesn't really surprise Levy since, she dryly points out, "as academics we spend our lives trying to get money to do research." When the firm decided to go public in 1986, Levy and Miller hit the road, selling their high-risk company to investment dealers and analysts unfamiliar with the fledgling biotechnology industry. "We were a great comedy team," says Levy, who actually enjoys the road shows. "We were really good. Jim would sell the dream and I would sell the product, the credibility." They didn't do too badly in that first go-round, raising $3 million at a price of $2.50 per share in their initial public offering on the Vancouver Stock Exchange.

Going public was an important learning experience and a challenge, says Levy. "You're so accountable once you've got investors' money in your bank account." They learned quickly that their enthusiasm and excitement over what they were doing led too easily to overpromising. "When you don't deliver," says Levy, "you suffer the results. Once the investors lose confidence, it takes a long time to build it back."

In the last five years, she says, they've worked hard to become very respectable — they don't overpromise. As well, they spend a lot of money with their PR firm. "That has paid off because our policy is, good news or bad, you inform the public about it as soon as possible and in a straightforward manner. If it's bad news, you take your hit and you put it behind you. You don't try to hide anything." The firm is, she says, "squeaky clean and that has paid off in terms of our credibility in the U.S. and Canada."

In fact, last year they moved into the U.S. market in an effort to raise $25 million but their story and reputation were so good, says Levy, that they raised $72 million. Today, their stock, with 26 million shares outstanding, is hovering around the $32 range, despite the fact that the company's first product has only just come to market, generating sales of $669,000 in 1996. The company is still not profitable — with expenses each year of $15 to $20 million, PHOTOFRIN will have to sell very well. Levy expects QLT to turn profitable in 1998.

Serendipity played a key role in turning QLT from start-up to establishment, according to Levy. At the same time as QLT began to focus on its second-generation photodynamic drug, a Johnson & Johnson subsidiary in the United States, PhotoMedica, was taking its first-generation photodynamic drug, called PHOTOFRIN, through clinical trials in humans. By chance, or, as Levy would say, serendipity, she was travelling to the University of Waterloo to give a speech. While there, she encountered outraged physicians whose supplies of PHOTOFRIN for clinical trials had been cut off. Even though the physicians were pleased with the trials, Johnson & Johnson had decided to pull out of photodynamic therapy and drop the trials.

"I suddenly had a wake-up call," says Levy. "We were going ahead with photodynamic therapy and here was PHOTOFRIN, already in the clinical trials. I thought maybe we should step in and at least try to do something about supplying this material to Canadian investigators." Miller, however, scoffed at such small thinking. He suggested buying PhotoMedica. Levy, who is cautious by nature, worried about the money to buy it but Miller brushed her hesitation aside and in October 1987 they acquired worldwide rights to PHOTOFRIN.

"There was so much serendipity going on," Levy says now. "American Cyanamid Co. [a huge U.S. pharmaceutical company] had been looking at QLT and both Cyanamid and Lederle Labs in the United States had been sniffing around photodynamic therapy for about six months. We all got together." QLT's expertise in photosensitizer research and Cyanamid's money and expertise in clinical development seemed like the ideal partnership to get PHOTOFRIN through the clinical tests and regulatory approvals. Then, too, Cyanamid gave QLT the cash and the credibility they needed to get onto the Toronto Stock Exchange, where they raised $10 million.

QLT has since formed a number of partnerships, relying on other firms such as U.S.-based Sanofi Winthrop and Beaufour Ipsen in France to market their product while QLT sticks to what they're good at — research and development. Levy is convinced that partnerships are the only way to operate in the complex and costly field of biotechnology but she's also learned, the hard way, that they can go awry, with near-devastating consequences.

"You're always at risk if you're in bed with an elephant and you're a mouse," says Levy. "They can roll over." That's what happened with American Cyanamid. In 1993, American Cyanamid, which was being bought out by American HomePatient Inc., decided not to invest any further in the research and development of QLT's second-generation light-sensitive drug, Benzoporphyrin derivative [BPD-MA]. For Levy, it was a frustrating setback — she needed another $100 million or so to get her drug tested, approved, and onto the market.

"It hurt us terribly in the public perception," says Levy, despite the fact that Cyanamid retained their rights to manufacture and sell PHOTOFRIN when it was ready for market and also remained, at that time, their largest shareholder. "The thing we've had to fight [since then] is that this technology [BPD-MA] doesn't work, because we were rejected by Cyanamid." Whereas, says Levy, it was QLT that wanted to proceed faster and that insisted on the restructuring so they could find a partner willing to invest in BPD-MA. "We needed to free ourselves to make other partnerships," she says.

Overcoming the public perception wasn't easy. "That's why the U.S. Food and Drug Administration [FDA] approval [for PHOTOFRIN] and the Sanofi relationship and the Beaufour Ipsen alliance are a vindication of the technology," she says. "All of these things attest to the value of the technology — these are great alliances that we now have."

QLT is wiser for the experience. "We've formed a credo now," says Levy. "When we form a partnership with another company the product we bring to that other company has to be just as important to them as it is to us. That's how we've forged our marketing relationships." Another thing they've learned — to make their partnerships extremely defined for specific areas, rather than a more global relationship as they had with Cyanamid.

Today, while QLT ultimately expects big things from its sales of PHOTOFRIN, which is just beginning to sell in Canada, the United States, Japan, and some European countries for the treatment of various kinds of cancer, it is their newer, second-generation drug, BPD-MA, which is more likely to bring the huge profits that QLT and its shareholders have long been awaiting.

BPD-MA is Levy's baby, based on the lab research that initially sparked her business gene and fuelled her drive to commercialize her research. In 1996, in partnership with CIBA Vision, a world leader in optical and ophthalmic research and products, QLT began final clinical trials in humans to prove the drug's effectiveness in treating age-related macular degeneration. This condition, known as AMD, causes blindness due to abnormal blood vessels leaking within the eye's retina. So far, the trials indicate that the drug can arrest the condition before further loss of vision occurs.

"The biggest professional thrill of my life was the first patient who received it," says Levy. "I got it into a patient and the patient responded. I can't tell you how exciting that moment is when you know you were there in the beginning and you've babysat it through a lot of aches and pains and now, it's there."

Finding a treatment, or possibly a cure, for AMD is particularly meaningful to Levy, who watched her vigorous mother go blind in her eighties from the disease, long before Levy thought of using her research to combat it. Now, ironically, it may be the product that puts QLT in the black.

"BPD-MA is probably going to be the blockbuster product that everyone hopes for," says Levy — if it receives regulatory approvals, which may be as soon as the year 2000. With as many as 200,000 elderly people in North America and Europe annually diagnosed with age-related macular degeneration, Levy says, "we think we'll capture a good part of that market rather quickly because there's no alternative treatment."

Levy's excitement over finally getting her own product to market derives more from her desire to make a difference in the world than to make big money, although she's always concerned about her shareholders. "Julia has great integrity," says Cairns. "She believes in what she's doing and has that in mind at all times. I've always had the impression that Julia wants to see the products succeed and be applied for what they can do for people, rather than build the company up and sell it off for a quick return or payback. She has her sights on the long-term potential of the product the company is making."

"Money isn't that important to me," agrees Levy. "I like money and I'm profligate in spending it, but it's never been the driving force." She has no idea exactly what her annual salary is ($300,000 plus bonus, according to company records) but thanks to her original shares and her stock options, she's already a millionaire. Galbraith says Levy doesn't care about the money. "We could probably stop paying her and she wouldn't notice," he quips.

When Levy is in the mood to spend money, she tends towards shopping sprees at Wear Else?, a popular Vancouver women's apparel store. Her lean frame favours Anne Klein clothes and shoes. When she gets the chance, she also likes to shop in New York's SoHo district, sometimes with her twenty-six-year-old daughter, Jennifer, who graduated recently from New York University Law School and now works as an advocate for the poor and the homeless in New York City. "Jennifer," says Levy proudly, "is really making a difference in the world."

Levy's two children, Jennifer and Benjamin, a thirty-five-year-old chef and restaurant owner with three children of his own, have always been her passion. Jennifer was just ten years old when Levy co-founded QLT but fortunately, the time-consuming business hours didn't really begin to eat into her life until about five years ago. While the children were growing up, she says, the time between dinner and their bedtime was theirs. "I'm quite good at compartmentalizing my life," she says. "It's the power of focus. It's like, when you're doing it, do it and don't get distracted. That's what made it possible for me."

It's a strategy she uses to this day. With her second husband, Edwin, a former professor of philosophy at UBC whom she married in 1969 and who is now involved in QLT's day-to-day activities as vice-president of corporate development, it's one way to avoid discussing business on weekends. "It's not constructive, intellectually," says Levy. "You end up obsessing about trivia."

Time management is another important strategy Levy uses to maintain balance in her life. She views anything that doesn't have a purpose as time-wasting. "It's devotion of time to a dedicated pastime or occupation," she says, which she applies to everything she does. "If you're going to relax, relax."

Levy finds relaxation several times each year at her remote Sonora Island cedar home, which can be reached only by the motorboat that's docked at Granville Island. Each weekend she battles her husband at tennis, which she says she's quite good at. An important pastime is reading, both fiction and non-fiction, and despite her hectic schedule, she reads at least one book a week, choosing her material from newspaper book reviews. Most recently, she read *Fugitive Pieces* by Anne Michaels. The topic interests her partially because her husband is Jewish and partially because her Dutch father, a banker, was taken prisoner by the Japanese in Indonesia during World War II.

Although Levy was born Julia Coppens in Singapore in 1934, she spent her early years in the Dutch East Indies until World War II broke out and her father sent her, her mother, and her sister to Vancouver, where an uncle lived. During the three-and-a-half years her father was held prisoner and after his return, Levy's mother worked as a physiotherapist to support the family, putting her daughters in elementary boarding school during weekdays. Her mother, says Levy, was the strength for the family; her father, she says, did work as an accountant but he had returned "a completely ruined man," traumatized by his experiences.

Although Levy experienced an unhappy childhood, when she felt out of place due to her higher-than-average intelligence and unusual background, she has not been disappointed by the rest of her life, despite a failed seven-year marriage. "I have a very good life," she says. "I think the insecurity of my background was certainly something that led me to say I have to be self-sufficient and succeed. I became very competitive with myself, more than anything." She's fortunate to have enjoyed good health and has a youthful outlook and attitude. "When you feel invigorated by what you do and energized by it, it shows in your face," she says.

Still, Levy hasn't quite reached her milestone — getting her own drug, BPD-MA, to market. And by the time QLT heads for regulatory approval in late 1998 for treatment of AMD, competition may not be too far behind them. Another firm, PDT Inc. in Santa Barbara, California, is currently testing its own photo-reactive drug, Tin Ethyl Etiopurpurin (SnET2) in combined phase one/two clinical trials for age-related macular degeneration. The company anticipates moving into phase three in 1998.

Levy, however, is unruffled. "Competition is out there, but we're in the lead." So far, QLT is still the only company with an approved photodynamic drug. "It's good to have competition," she says. "It shows that it's real."

3 FLYING HIGH

ADELE FOGLE

By Laura Pratt

The air under the fishing-line-dangling model airplanes is filled with talk of T-33s, 101 Bolingbrooks, and gaskets. Loud, variously coveralled, and asmudge in a film of grease, the flying men gather in the airport lounge for a coffee and story exchange. Hardly the place for a lady. You have to go to the highest reaches of the executive offices to find female blood at the Guelph Airpark.

Adele Fogle is the president of Aviation International Canada Ltd., a flying school and airplane charter and maintenance business operating out of the Guelph Airpark, on the outskirsts of Guelph, an hour's drive west of Toronto. Her painted nails double the length of her fingers, her hair is an elegant ringer for a movie star's, and her make-up is more suited to the stateroom than the stratosphere. Fogle works out with a personal trainer three days a week at a gym and tops that off with regular sessions of karate and downhill skiing. She wears as much leather as a cattle farm, and she picks from a Ferrari and a Range Rover when she drives to work each morning. "When you get in a little airplane, and go somewhere, and come back," she whispers, in a voice borrowed from Marilyn Monroe, "nobody can say, 'You see, I told you so.' Or 'Do this.' Or 'Go here.' When I fly, it's the ultimate high. And I couldn't have believed, in my wildest dreams, that I would ever be able to do something like this."

When Adele was a little girl growing up in an apartment building on Toronto's Palmerston Boulevard, with her sister, Ruth, and parents Norma and Harry Englander, her dreams took flight from the couch in the dining room-cum-bedroom she shared with her big sister and grandmother. Her folks spoke Russian in the home, a practice that embarrassed Adele immensely and dissuaded her from inviting many friends home. It was just as well: home was tight quarters for extras. In their family, money was scarce and seemed even scarcer as end-of-war economics sent the families of Adele's friends uptown, and towards prosperity, while the Englanders lagged behind. "My father was not that kind of guy, so our standard of living did not change." When her mother needed three yards of fabric, she'd buy two and a half. She subscribed, her daughter explains, to the Jewish concept of *fergin*. She denied herself things, because she felt she didn't deserve them. But her daughter couldn't suffer the same deprivation. "I always wanted things," Fogle says.

It's her great regret that her story — the one that details the accumulation of those "wanted things" — really doesn't begin until she was in her late thirties, with her two daughters in school and time on her hands. "You waste so much of your good life saying you can't do things," she despairs. "I'm sorry I didn't go to university. I'm sorry I didn't have a career when I was young, that I opted to get married because that was what I thought I was supposed to do. And then, all of a sudden, you reach forty. Your kids are bigger, and you say, 'Why can't I learn to fly?'" Why indeed. At age twenty, Adele married Arnold Fogle in 1954. So this self-described career housewife who lived a quiet life with her husband and school-age daughters, Corrine and Susan, off the affluent Bridle Path in Toronto, tagged along one day with a male neighbour who was heading for a flying lesson. "I was petrified," she recalls of her first hours on her learning craft, a Cessna 150. "I also thought that my instructor was a genius because he was able to find his way back to the airport." Two years later, when she was forty, Fogle earned her own licence and instructor's rating.

Today, this sixty-three-year-old grandmother of two flies airplanes for fun and profit. She says hanging in the heavens in one of those small planes is like sitting in a movie theatre, watching a panorama unfold below her. Her first international aviation competition was a race from New York to Paris in 1986, an experience that exhilarated her and threw her ambitions wide to the heavens. In 1994, she entered a round-the-world air race as part of a four-woman team. The trip took twenty-eight days and included stops in Morocco, Turkey, Dubai, India, Vietnam, Japan, Russia, and the United States. Although they weren't among the first teams to cross the finish line, Fogle and her flying partners were proud to have been one of only two groups of women to enter — and complete — the arduous course. Last spring, she and her flying partner — seventy-three-year-old Daphne Schiff, whom she'd met when she joined the international organization of women pilots, the 99s — competed in a race around South America. The races, Fogle marvels, have been tough. The long-range tanks on their plane carried about nine hours of fuel (rather than the usual three). In pursuit of the next designated stop, teams would race for as long as their fuel would allow them. If they couldn't make it, their stops to refuel would have to take place during a running clock.

But Fogle's take-off was not immediately successful. "I had gotten my licence, but I couldn't get a job," she remembers. "They looked at this forty-year-old housewife and said, 'Who wants her as a flight instructor?' And so I went into my own business."

On the wall of Fogle's wood-panelled office, just this side of the wind sockets fingering the breeze, a copy of the Sunday *Item-Tribune* from July 4, 1937, trumpets: "Believe Amelia Safe on Island." Behind her desk, shelves buckle under a propeller, a collection of flight instruments, and a frying pan with "Around the World Air Race 1994" printed on its back. There's also a placard that reads "One of the greatest labour-saving inventions of today is tomorrow" on one side, and "Gone Flying" on the other. All around, yellowing newspaper articles celebrate the unusual species that Fogle successfully worked to become: a woman pilot who, incidentally, also runs her own airport.

Her first venture was in partnership with a pair of earthbound cops who liked the idea of managing a small flight-training school in King City, Ontario. Fogle met the cops through a former flying instructor and offered to give them the first 100 hours of her flight time for nothing. "They had no budget," she shrugs. "That's why I got the job." After a few months, the unpaid employee became a partner when the cops decided to get into the charter business and Fogle chipped in on a twin-engine six-seater Aztec. They removed the back four seats and won a contract hauling mail to Montreal every night, then waiting for the newspapers to come off the presses because it was too expensive to come home to Toronto empty-handed. Since her partners weren't pilots, Fogle did a lot of the late-night flying — an experience, she recalls, that was alternately beautiful and lonely.

Less than a year later, the construction company that owned the airport's land bought out a neighbouring printing company and announced it needed the air strip to park its trucks. "When the guys were given notice, they were delighted because they didn't like the business anyway; they weren't entrepreneurs." But by then, Fogle was flying high and keen to find another place to land. "I didn't want to get out of business," she says. "I was just getting into business. My kids were both away in high school. I got married when I was twenty, I didn't have a chance at a career. I really wanted to do something. When this came along, I was just so happy to have my own identity, to be able to get up and do something out of the house that was just mine."

In fact, Fogle's mother was the first female entrepreneur of the family. And hers, too, was a career launched in life's second half. She had come to Canada from Russia when she was a teenager, and she couldn't read or write English. The family was desperately poor, so she had to find work in a factory. As a young woman, she married Adele's father, a furrier who, according to his daughter, "wasn't terribly successful." Adele's mother helped out by underlining coats with a black muslin layer she sewed onto the back of the skins. It was painstaking work that had to be done by hand, and other furriers soon began dropping by to ask if she would perform the same task for them. When her husband's business failed, she opened up a small shop in the corner of a manufacturer's facility. After that, she established her own dress store, Nora-Lee, in the west end of Toronto and, boasts her daughter, did very well. "She was a very 'people' person, a real hands-on entrepreneur. I didn't give her credit when she was alive for doing what she did."

Fogle's mother was ambitious to have her daughters educated and to have them learn the piano in the style of her brothers, who were concert musicians. She was ambitious for her daughters to be self-sufficient, to marry nice men, and to have children. But she was not ambitious for them to have jobs of their own. "Her ambitions weren't what I ended up to be," says Adele.

Fogle never told her mother about her flying. When she was thirty, and decided to try skiing, her mother told her a woman with two kids shouldn't ski, and that she'd be sorry when she broke her leg. When Fogle broke her leg ten years later and had to call for help, she *was* sorry. She'd expected more than an "I told you so" from her mother. As for her kids, well, "they thought I was nuts anyway."

The Maple Airport, northwest of Toronto, had already been purchased by land developers with plans to build houses in a year or two when Fogle took it over in 1986. What's more, the operation was on the verge of bankruptcy. When Fogle asked the airport manager if she might rent the space, he said he'd be "delighted" and handed it over for a song. Still, Fogle, who had paid the cops for two-thirds of everything in King City, needed to acquire some operating capital, a requirement that sent her headlong into the most unpleasant territory for women in business — the bank. When she asked the bank manager for a $25,000 loan, he phoned her husband to ask if it would be all right with him if they gave her one. "It was a mistake mentioning that my husband banked there," Fogle says, the memory distorting her delicate features. "And it was the only time I made it. It made me so angry, though, because it was difficult enough for me to do this. I don't know where I got the nerve to all of a sudden walk into a world that I knew nothing about, a man's world, full of licences and regulations."

Just the same, Fogle spent the money patching the runways of that man's world and leasing a couple more airplanes. Eventually, she purchased a twin-engine Cessna 172. In the office, the toilets needed fixing, everything needed painting, and she bought a lot of plants to brighten the place. What's more, Fogle took over management of the airport's flight school and learned the ropes of the tie-down business the facility also maintained (tie-downs are planes owned by private individuals leasing an airport's space to park). Fuel was the biggest expense at Maple Neiltown Air ("When Esso comes and puts $30,000 worth of fuel in the ground, you've got to pay them"), along with payroll and parts. Planes need new engines every 1,800 flying hours. In the summer, she hired someone to cut her grass. When winter hit, she realized someone else was going to have to clear the runways of snow. "All of this was news to me."

News to her also were the incensed creditors who stalked the place from the first day, in search of monies owed from the previous manager. "That was my first foray into the business world. I didn't owe them money, but I was a new company operating out of that facility." At first, she admits, she panicked. "But with every day you get stronger. I learned to say, 'It's not my problem. Sue him. Leave me alone.'" The guys she encountered on the job, and there were plenty, left her alone, too. They regarded Fogle as a bit of an oddity: an older woman with a thing for flying. But the trick she discovered early on was not to care what anyone thought.

Fogle put in a solid bank of hours at her Maple business, and delegation didn't work out too well. On the weekends, a student opened the airport for her, but one Sunday when she phoned at 7 a.m., there was no answer. By the time she got there, a line-up was snaking down the tarmac. "Every day," she says of that period, "there was another trauma."

She built the business by word of mouth along with a highly successful roadside sign campaign advertising flight training gift certificates but, when the developers moved in two years later, Fogle left with no regrets. "It was almost like a graveyard when I first got there. Transport Canada didn't know me and certainly didn't take me seriously. They weren't user friendly, nor were they female-user friendly. They made things difficult for me. I didn't know what 'old boys' meant until I got to be in business. There was no old girls' network in the flying business at that time. By the time I left, it was a busy, busy school — a couple of hundred clients, maybe more. And, by the end, Transport Canada sure knew who I was."

But progress is an uneven creature. Fogle and her husband belong to a private golf club that's very male-oriented and allows women to play only at prescribed times. When she came back from the around-the-world race just ahead of a tailwind of press, the president of the golf course approached her to say the club was proud, and that it was so wonderful she'd done this great thing. Fogle asked whether that meant she could play golf on Saturday mornings. The president didn't know what to say. "He just walked away."

Others greeted her by announcing that they, too, had flown around the world and had enjoyed the experience immensely. A vision of misplaced elegance among the grease monkeys, the pilot doesn't resent the misunderstanding. "Why would anybody think I actually flew around the world?"

Through a tip-off from a former Maple client, Fogle was offered the chance to buy into a school at Guelph Airpark in 1988, and, with the little bit of profit she'd earned at Maple, she grabbed it, along with two partners. Including four airplanes, the school cost about $300,000. In 1991, she bought the pair out by mortgaging a piece of property she'd owned for years. In its early days, the place was bare bones. Fogle fixed up the restaurant and existing classroom, built another classroom, and purchased some new equipment. She also bought out the fellow who was employed doing field maintenance and established her own maintenance business. Maintenance, she says, is the heart of the school. Without it, popularity of the school notwithstanding, she couldn't make any money.

"For many years, it was hand to mouth," she recalls. "I had to keep putting my own money in to meet my payroll." When she first arrived in Guelph, Fogle hooked up with the Royal Bank. Squeezing money from that institution was like squeezing a stone, but she doesn't blame the bank. Times were tough then, she concedes, and hers was a tough business to succeed in. "It's easy to blame the banks, but the banks will come through if they know you're dedicated. You have to be aware of what you're doing. You have to be dedicated and willing to stick your chin out. And you have to be willing to let people laugh at you, because they're going to." Still, after her partners left, getting and keeping a line of credit proved more of a challenge than it should have — "because they were men, and I was the woman left behind." Sometimes, Fogle would phone her bank manager and plead for a spot loan, just $500 to get her through the weekend. He would refuse, because she was almost always at her limit. If she became $100 overdrawn, he would phone her and demand the money. Theirs was a tight and oppressive relationship. But in March 1996, it was this very same bank manager who nominated her for the Woman Entrepreneur of the Year award. "I was so honoured, because of the fighting for so many years."

Fogle called her business Aviation International in order to attract foreign students in pursuit of a much-respected Canadian flying licence. In the early 1990s, things started to turn around for Fogle and Aviation International. In 1996, she did more than $1 million in business. She employs some thirty people, depending on the season, including ten full-time instructors. All told, Fogle owns and operates thirteen airplanes, among them five Cessna 150s, which are two-seaters and the easiest plane to fly. She has a flight simulator, where students do a lot of their on-ground training; two runways, each with two directions; and fifty hangars, which are rented to owners of private airplanes. Her lease stipulates that she is the only person on the field who can do maintenance. She owns the fuel tanks, sells the fuel, and operates the restaurant, a part of her interests she recently handed over to a partner to run. In southern Ontario, there isn't a lot of competition in the flight instruction trade any more: just Buttonville, Brampton, Kitchener/Waterloo, and a scattering of tiny schools. She figures Aviation International is the third largest in the area.

Because she's a woman, Fogle says her business values are different from those of her competition. "I really care about the people who work for me. I wouldn't in any way verbally or emotionally abuse anybody. I wouldn't just fire anybody unless I had really good cause. Women are caretakers and caregivers." Loyalty is the biggest thing she looks for in the people she hires.

Her biggest mistakes, she reveals with a broad grin, have revolved around hiring the wrong people and giving authority to people who shouldn't have had it. "I'm not a mechanic — that's the only thing I really don't know how to do — so if my mechanic tells me I need this or that, I've got to trust him. I can't go down to the hangar and count the bolts every weekend." And Fogle says she would never have partners again unless she could find somebody "who had the exact same goals, the same level of commitment, the same pockets as I have, who was willing to risk the same as I am. I would have to find somebody like me. But somebody like me would probably not get along with me. And I would not be a partner with a man, because I think women try too hard to please men, and that's difficult." (The restaurant, she says, is a different story. "It's my Achilles' heel. I've tried to run it myself, and there's no way anyone can ever make money in that place.")

All company employees are on a profit-sharing plan. Fogle says, "I pay good salaries and I've got a few very loyal, very key employees." Eight years ago, a stay-at-home mother came to work for her as a dispatcher, and now she pretty much manages everything for Fogle while she's away, tearing up personal skies. The business is in good hands, Fogle says, so she's free to drift off when she pleases. But retirement isn't a consideration, at least not until "my brain goes dead."

Aviation International's main focus is flight training, and it teaches every stage from *ab initio,* or beginner, through to airline transport of pilot's licence (ATPL). Most of Fogle's students, after earning their commercial licences, go on to get their instructor's rating so they can make some money teaching while banking the hours required to become a commercial pilot. Fogle gives many of her candidates instructor jobs. The school attracts students from all over the world and, every summer for the past four, it's been awarded the Air Cadet contract, which sees sixteen of the fifty-six Ontario Air Cadets who've been awarded pilot-licence training scholarships spending six weeks at Fogle's facility. She also teaches recreational students, men and women who are following through on lifelong ambitions to learn to fly. These ones are mostly in their fifties and are after private licences so they can tool around the skies with the abandon of youth.

More and more of Fogle's students are women, partly a reason for, and partly a reflection of, their increased acceptance in the field. "When I started, I was very uncomfortable in the whole aviation environment," Fogle recalls. "The instructors would look at me as if to say, 'What are you doing here? You don't belong here.' I felt very old and intimidated by the experience. I remember when I used to go for my flying lesson, my instructor would tell me to go out and walk around the airplane — and he'd sit in the lounge and have a coffee. And then we'd just go. He wouldn't tell me what he was doing or why. And then he'd say goodbye and walk away. Now, you sit down in the classroom with the instructor and do preparatory flight instruction — what are we going to do today and how are we going to do it. You do your flight and then come back and have a debriefing during which your instructor tells you what you're going to do on your next flight, so you're prepared. But when it was me who was the student, I was so intimidated by this new environment that, when the instructor would bring me back and walk away, I'd think he didn't want to fly with me, and I'd be scared to even book another lesson."

Everywhere, forces were working against Adele Fogle climbing to the heights she dared. "Everyone and everything" tried to discourage her from dreaming big, she says. When the Maple venture began to crumble, one of her partners, on his way out the door, asked why she didn't just declare bankruptcy. "I said I couldn't do that." Even Arnold, Fogle's husband of forty-three years, has visited his wife's playground only a handful of times. He's not interested in aviation, she says. "The most support he ever gave me was not standing in my way." And many of her friends never believed she could pull the crazy airport thing off. They wouldn't come up with her for years, Fogle says, because they weren't "going to fly with that dingaling." Once, after she was nominated for Entrepreneur of the Year, Fogle told a couple she knew about the honour over dinner. The man chuckled and winked at Arnold. "How much did it cost your husband?" he asked. So what kept her going in the face of all this adversity? "It's just the way I am."

Today, the way she is is head of a million-dollar-plus business whose success she partly credits to integration. The flying business, she says, is only one facet: fuel, outside maintenance, and chartering are other profit centres. And Fogle feels lucky for being in a business that trains professionals for an industry starting to cry out for them. "A couple of years ago, you couldn't buy or steal a job in aviation. Now the airlines are starting to feel a shortage of pilots, and they're hiring them from the commuters. The commuters get their pilots from the couriers, the couriers get their pilots from the instructors, and it filters right back to the flying schools."

Because Fogle's mother worked so hard, she was able to send her two children to camp in the summer to save them from hanging out on the streets. Camp Muskoka turned out to be a seasonal retreat for kids from well-to-do families, and it proved to be young Adele's introduction to the affluent class. When school started again, camp friends invited her to their homes, and she would peek into their well-appointed bedrooms, observe their shiny cars, and be served by their maids. "I would aspire to that," she says. "I'm not a quitter and, when I start something, I have to continue it. Sometimes I'd wonder, why am I doing this? But there's just something in me that wouldn't let me stop."

Today, Fogle surveys her achievements with reserve and humility. She lives a "lavish lifestyle" in North Toronto doing what she wants to do, whenever it suits her to do it. She travels frequently, including a recent biking trip through Vietnam with her daughter, Corrine, thirty-seven. She enjoys her fancy cars. And she has far too many clothes and shoes. "But I never get dressed up to come to work. I always just wear ordinary pants, and no jewellery because I don't think it's appropriate. I hope I don't flaunt anything, because I don't think it makes a difference. I take a great deal of pride in my house, because I didn't grow up in a nice house. Every time I come home at night, I look around and think how lucky I am. I never take anything for granted."

But she says success is a matter of perspective. Fogle's eldest daughter, Susan Michelle, died in 1995 when she was only thirty-eight. And it's less the material wealth she reflects upon when measuring her achievements. This summer, the woman whose maiden initials matched those of her latter-day hero, Amelia Earhart, was honoured with a plaque in the Earhart-dedicated "Forest of Friendship" in Atchison, Kansas. Flying, she says, gave her a purpose she'd never had. "I was a stay-at-home mom, my husband was building a business, he wasn't home a lot. When I became a pilot, went into flying, started to race, that began to fulfil a need for me. Before that, I was the kids' mother, I was Arnie's wife. Now, I was a person for me. All of a sudden, I started to evolve."

4 REACHING FOR THE STARS

ROSINA BUCCI, NADIA RONA, VERA MILLER

By Rosa Harris-Adler

Not shown: Rosina Bucci

I n an old sandstone office building on St. Laurent Boulevard, the trendy strip of Montreal turf known to locals as The Main, the casting offices of Elite Productions are as busy as the streets seven storeys below. Restless actors, extras, and wannabes constantly circulate in the narrow hall that serves as a reception area, itching for that breakthrough film, TV, or commercial role they know Elite can give them. Others sit in one of the many aluminum and brown Naugahyde chairs of mass-produced vintage, chairs that seem to come from central casting themselves.

On the walls are posters that testify to the accomplishments of Montreal's top anglophone casting agency: *The Boys of St. Vincent, Blind Fear, Wild Thing, Choices, Criminal Law, Malarek*. In the middle of the long wall hangs a large recent magazine cover of Elite's founding partners: Rosina Bucci, forty-five, and identical twins Nadia Rona and Vera Miller, fifty-eight, the "Master Casters."

From behind one of the doors come muffled sounds of conversation, then an inordinately loud "...And there's nothing around for a thousand miles!" A young bearded man emerges from the room, puts on his coat, and leaves. A moment later, an Elite employee, a dark-haired young man with his own matinee-idol looks, strides out of the room and summons one of the two jeans-clad hopefuls in the reception area.

In the midst of it all, a curious Dalmatian wanders up, sniffing and looking for a pat. Two more dogs are meandering around and another is napping in the middle of the floor. The Dalmatian soon departs with his owner, a tall, middle-aged woman who is, as it turns out, an agent.

Overhead, the ten-foot-high ceiling is painted black, the exposed pipes decorated in lighter colours. The office space is bright, lit by winter sun streaming through large windows that frame an imposing view of Mount Royal. Beneath the windows, Rosina Bucci, dark and vivacious, with expressive, gripping eyes and a warm smile, sits at her desk speaking animatedly into the phone between bites of pizza. In another corner, Vera Miller is glued to the phone as well, her computer screen lit with lines of numbers; twin Nadia Rona sits at a nearby desk, riffling through files. The sisters, with bobbed blonde waif-like hair and broad mischievous smiles, are what used to be described as pert. All three wear comfortable sweaters and pants — Nadia and Vera in similar but not identical gear. Rosina is the most fashionable in a red chenille pullover, skin-tight black leggings, and high heels. This is the nerve centre of Elite Productions, an enterprise that generates more than $300,000 in revenue annually.

Nadia acknowledges the chaos — and seems grateful for it.

"We used to have bigger premises next door," she says in her musical Slovak accent, "but back in 1992 and 1993, business slumped badly. Not many companies were shooting films in Montreal and we were really concerned about how we were going to pay the rent. So we re-evaluated and moved here. Of course, the moment we did, business picked up again and now we're a bit cramped. In the past couple of years, we haven't had too much slack. Still, we're not going to move again. It's not just the rent — it's the business tax, too: your overhead goes *way* up. We're staying here."

If Nadia speaks like the hard-nosed veteran of a recession or two, she has good reason. Since she and her partners incorporated Elite in 1983, their stint in the capricious world of show business has endured a lot of ups and downs. Nonetheless, to hear them tell it, they had no choice but to persist. Theatre, all three say with an absence of melodrama, is their destiny.

The twins were born to Edith and David Debnai in the Slovak town of Bratislava in 1939. After the war, in the tense atmosphere that prevailed as the Soviet grip tightened on their country, the girls diverted themselves by staging plays for their friends and going to "lots and lots of movies." They longed to become screen stars and dreamed of Hollywood.

Reality brought them to Canada. Just before the iron curtain fell, the family immigrated here because a friend had said there were good business opportunities. Once settled, their father launched a successful paint and adhesive company. A pragmatist, he also laid down the law — no theatre training for his daughters — and nudged them towards more practical careers in business.

"He felt acting was fine as a hobby," Nadia recalls, "but he insisted that we have a *real* profession. So we took a two-year course at a local business college, where we learned accounting, among other things, and we worked in business afterward."

Still, they couldn't quench their thirst for the stage — it was as though theatre "was embedded in our bodies and minds at a very young age," says Vera — and they began to attend classes at the Actor's Studio in the 1970s, a school and workshop with a solid reputation in Montreal for training up-and-comers. There, they met Bucci, an Italian-born English teacher and systems analyst who also loved theatre. Rosina was a baby when she came to Canada with her family after the war in 1951; her father worked as a factory foreman and her mother as a seamstress. "I can't completely explain my attraction to the stage," she says now. "You can't explain passion — it just *is*."

The twins first worked with Rosina when she directed them in a number of plays at the studio. "Soon, all three of us got involved after hours, helping in the office, interviewing new students," says Nadia. "Eventually, we decided we didn't like the way they were running the theatre."

Elite was born out of this conviction that they were outgrowing the Actor's Studio and the time seemed right to test themselves. Vera's daughter and Nadia's two sons were teenagers and Rosina, married in 1975, has no children. Looking for new challenges, the three decided to form a company to produce dinner theatre in Montreal. The Hyatt hotel had just closed down its nightclub and had a big empty space "begging to be filled," as Rosina puts it. Cocky and naïve, the threesome proposed to the manager that they run a dinner theatre in the space. Much to their amazement, he agreed — and they panicked. Each partner then borrowed $1,000 from their businessman husbands to put up the money to create Elite and to produce their first play, *Eat Your Heart Out.* But there were no deep pockets to bail them out if they failed. Nadia's husband, Peter Rona, owns a company that makes interactive entertainment for computers. Vera's mate, Hy Miller, once ran a chemical paint company; he's now retired. Rosina's husband, Tony Green, is a record producer. But back then all were still making their way, smack-dab in the middle of the middle class.

No one thought they'd make it, including their backer-spouses, who argued they just didn't know enough about producing. "We didn't," chuckles Nadia now. "We didn't even know how important it was to have a stage manager because we really didn't fully understand what one did. But we were lucky. We met up with and hired a local director, Terry Donald. He was a big help. He told us what we'd need in terms of lighting, props, and sets and where to go for what. But most of our experience was directly on the job."

In spite of it all, the show was a smash and they mounted twelve more productions over the next two years. The work was exhausting and demanding, requiring long hours of dealing with scripts and directors, egos and artistes, but the partners were making a name for themselves in the process.

Rosina laughs as she recalls some of the problems they encountered during their trial by fire. "Each one of us was involved in every aspect of each production at the beginning," she says, "and there were some terrifying moments. I remember one opening night when the audience was already filing in and the set designers were still painting the scenery. Another time, one of our lead actors tore a ligament playing tennis and had to do the rest of the show in a cast. There have been costumes that have disappeared at the last minute and broken props. There was always something going desperately wrong. But we'd pull it together somehow."

Meanwhile, movie producer Pieter Kroonenberg, a friend from the Actor's Studio days, asked Elite to help him find extras for a film he was working on, *Cross-Country,* directed by Paul Lynch. So they began a side venture in casting. "We got into it at the right time, just when film companies were starting to do a lot of shooting in Montreal because of tax breaks the government was giving," says Rosina. "And we had a good formula with the three of us. We were all knowledgeable. Nadia and Vera had their business training and I had worked a little bit for another casting director before we joined forces. We knew the acting community in Montreal very well between us, so we put our heads together."

The dinner-theatre business continued to grow until 1985 when they encountered their first setbacks — a string of what Nadia calls, without mincing words, flops.

"There was one show called *Up Your Alley* that just didn't work," she says, "and there was another one in Toronto with Kaye Ballard, but it wasn't mounted in the right theatre. And at that point we lost a lot of money, about $80,000. But we never went into debt. We were able to finance our losses through our casting. And that's when we decided we'd never produce for ourselves again. We'd produce for someone else for a fee. But we wouldn't put our own money into it."

During those first lean years, the partners took no salaries, sinking whatever little money they made back into the business. They concede their plight was made easier by the fact that they had other sources of income — modest private assets in real estate and supportive mates — which allowed them to keep going, too.

"On the other hand, there were times when our company has been more successful than some of our husbands' businesses," says Rosina. "None of us has ever viewed it as a competition. We've married pretty understanding men, by and large."

That encouragement and forbearance on the home front, say all three, provided each with a calm port in the unpredictable climate of the entertainment business. In all cases, their marriages endured.

"They never say to us: 'What time are you going to be home?' because they understand that in show business, sometimes you have to work long hours," says Nadia. "My husband doesn't make time demands on me nor do I on him. Rosina's husband is a record producer with a studio not far from our offices, so he understands the entertainment industry really well. And as for Vera's husband, well, because he's retired he does all the shopping and cooking — for both of us. He calls and says, 'What do you want for dinner?' and he even sends us lunch."

All three partners insist they rarely fight seriously among themselves. They credit their mutual respect and their complementary natures as the key to getting past their differences. They divide the chores equally, each taking charge of a particular project but working in close consultation with the other two.

"The fact that two of us are identical twins helps because we really do think alike," laughs Vera, who is the one primarily responsible for accounting. "We trust one another enough not to worry about who spends what and where. And our personalities blend well together. We're all very outgoing and able to deal with the public." What's more, their joint experience in theatre is a major asset to their business, says Nadia. "If I get stuck and can't think what actor to bring in," she points out, "I don't have to worry about it all on my own. Somebody else will have an idea. We're three casting directors in one."

Often they rely on instincts. Elite was given the task of casting all fifty roles in the highly acclaimed feature *The Boys of St. Vincent,* the harrowing story of childhood abuse in an institution. The lead, Johnny Morina, had no previous experience, but his lack of acting credentials didn't stop them from taking the risk.

"It's exciting when we discover young talent like that," says Nadia. "When someone trying out for a role walks into a room, our intuition goes to work. We can usually tell before even starting the audition if this person has a chance. It's not only in the way they look. It's the way they present themselves. That's not something you can teach anyone."

That intuition, they maintain, is one of the characteristics that makes their work particularly suited to women. "It's not just a matter of spotting talent," Vera elaborates. "It's also a matter of determining if a person is right for a particular role. And I think women are at an advantage when it comes to trusting their feelings on something like that." Adds Nadia, "There are more women than men in this business and I think that's in part because it's intuition-based. You can't learn this industry at a university. But along with intuition, you need general business knowledge and you have to understand the industry insideout. You need to know who's out there, which actors are in which cities, what they cost, who their agents are. Ninety percent of what we do is artistic. But we are also negotiators and you have to have a feel for that too, when you're making deals with agents, producers, and actors all the time."

Part of their work, says Vera, is soothing the notoriously fragile egos of actors and instilling confidence in newcomers who see the three as surrogate mothers. "You have to be very diplomatic and even-tempered to handle our clientele," she explains. "Emotions are an actor's trade. Many are used to exploring them openly. But that can make for fireworks. We've learned, over the years, how to cajole and comfort, but it isn't always easy."

As the interview progresses, a variety of characters comes and goes, filling out application forms, answering casting calls, gossiping about new productions. One young man with ripped-knee jeans and a winter jacket is auditioning; another, neatly dressed with close-cropped hair, is picking up a paycheque. Then there's a grizzled old fellow, wearing a tweed fedora and a long plaid scarf over a fisherman-knit sweater. He looks like a homeless man hoping for a gig as an extra, but he's probably a character actor. Another middle-aged executive type, neatly coiffed and wearing a three-piece navy suit, pink shirt, and burgundy tie, looks more like a banker than the aspiring actor he is. The golden Labrador retriever and the black Lab who complete the scenario belong to Nadia and her daughter, but it isn't uncommon for Rosina's dog, a Bouvier, to also put in an appearance. Telephone calls, intercom messages, and ongoing business by-play further add to the turmoil as the partners reminisce.

Now they're talking about the rough years of the early nineties when the Quebec government partially rescinded the liberal tax laws that had previously encouraged so much American film activity in the province. Elite survived, say the partners, not only because they made some tough decisions but because of the nature of their work.

Aside from the move to smaller digs, "we had to lay off some people and put them on unemployment," Vera recalls now. "Every day we wondered if we were going to make it. We cut our own salaries again because we had no choice. But because we're essentially a service company, we couldn't get into too much debt. We didn't have inventory that we have to worry about. We didn't really have suppliers as such — phone, rent, long-distance calls. No question, it's very nerve-racking to be running behind on the rent, but we managed."

What helped, they say, is their decision five years ago to start a Toronto office of Elite. As business fell off in Montreal, it took off in their new location, easing their mounting expenses. There was no breakthrough contract, they say, to tell them they'd finally made it — just a slow and steady building of a trusting clientele. This year, Bucci will spend nine months in Canada's biggest city casting for a new television series "Once A Thief." She's not looking forward to all the back-and-forth travel her assignment in Toronto will require, but all acknowledge it's part of the reality of success. At one time, they even considered opening an office in Vancouver, too, but quashed the idea: no one liked the prospect of commuting.

"When people hire us, they hire *us*," Nadia explains. "They don't want to work with anyone else. So it's not like you can branch out anywhere you want. You've got to be there. And we couldn't be. So there are limits to how much you can expand."

The partners say they are in a highly competitive business — there are fourteen casting companies in Quebec alone — but add that there is honour among rivals. In the early days, they had to contend with fly-by-night agencies who would promote the actors they represented for a fee to producers they also charged. But a self-policing casting association was subsequently established and that contributed to the industry's professionalism. It created standards, setting guidelines for conflict of interest, ethics, and fees for services rendered. Today, Elite occasionally even consults with other casting directors because each agency tends to have its own roster of clients and talent and they can all trade leads when it's useful.

"When someone new starts up, there's often a bit of a kerfuffle among the rest of us," says Rosina, "but once the dust settles, especially during a busy period, we all tend to have our own clients. Every once in a while, of course, there'll be a shift of clientele and that can be stressful. A project will come along that everyone wants, but it's friendly competition. And we have our mainstays — there are at least three or four major clients who do a lot of films who always hire us."

They say it's never been a problem reconciling their artistic natures with the practical demands of their work. For the twins, it's a legacy of their father's insistence on business school. And Rosina says of herself, "I've always dreamed in Technicolor, but I've always been grounded, too. It's a balance that seems to come naturally."

The women employ a full-time staff of four, one of whom is Nadia's daughter, Linda, thirty-five, who casts most of the extras. Another employee serves as cameraman and acts as Elite's representative on the set. A third assists in the main casting and books commercials. The receptionist is the fourth. Junior staff members earn minimum wage as they learn the craft, but the upbeat atmosphere suggests they're happy to have their feet in the door of an industry often perceived as glamorous.

It *is* glamorous, all three admit. They've rubbed shoulders with stars like Robert de Niro, Nick Nolte, Liza Minnelli, and Bruce

Willis. Although they're rarely responsible for casting these big names, when work on a production begins, they often meet with the leads. They still sound a little star-struck when they talk about meeting Richard Chamberlain, an early idol of all three. But they're generally blasé about the big names now.

"Some are nice and some are not so nice. Sure, there is certainly some glamour — we get to go to all the theatre openings for free and a lot of parties with stars — but the day-to-day work is work," says Rosina. "One person we eventually let go basically came out and said, 'I can't answer the phone and greet people at the same time. It's too much work.' She wanted to be sitting in on casting sessions and deciding who did a better audition, and, sure, that's the fun part. But you have to do all the work prior to that to earn the right to get to that point."

The agency makes all its money by charging producers and directors $1,200 on average to cast a commercial and $10,000 or more to cast a role in a feature film; the price tends to go up, say the partners, the more roles they have to cast because the research is more intensive. Often they will cast everything but the starring roles in movies. As a starting point, the agency searches its office data base of prospective actors.

"We can find an actor by age, weight, height — whatever — and I don't think anyone else does this," says Nadia. "If you want someone who's five foot two or three, or a blonde with blue eyes, we'll locate an appropriate candidate."

At the turn of a new millennium, Elite seems relatively secure in a notoriously volatile industry. The partners acknowledge it wasn't always thus, but say they would do it again — and they encourage other women to venture forth.

"Of course you have to do the logical thing, like making sure there's a market for your service or product, researching what it will cost you and so forth," says Rosina. "But it's almost more important to be sure it's what you want — and that you really love the field you're entering." Vera adds that it helps to start small. "Make sure you know what it's going to take financially," she advises, "then build slowly and your confidence will follow." Nadia echoes, "You have to make your own destiny. If you want it badly enough, it'll happen. You just need the basic determination to do what you want to do."

As she talks, a pretty young woman dons a vintage fur coat and a porkpie hat and heads for the door. As she swings her backpack in place, the receptionist congratulates her on getting the part. "Yes, it's a nice birthday present," smiles the young actor as she leaves, the door creaking on its hinges as it closes.

5 PROVIDING THE BEST **CARE**

PAT BEST

By Laura Pratt

ANDREW DANSON

On the bulletin board in Pat Best's office in Orangeville, Ontario, there's a pinned-up copy of that clichéed illustration of a woman who looks, alternately, like a very old hag and a fresh young thing, depending on how she catches your eye. It's all a matter of perception. And Best has suffered at the hands of perception all the latter years of her life. Today, Best is the founder and adminis- trator of Séan-Lee Community Nursing Agency Ltd., a home health- care provider with offices in Orangeville, Midland, and Owen Sound, Ontario. She employs seventy-five registered nurses, registered prac- tical nurses, health-care aides and homemakers who put in about 1,500 part-time hours a week caring for ailing clients in their own homes. Increasingly early discharges from hospitals and widespread cost-cutting measures have seen the emphasis for health care shift from within to without medical institutions. This means Best and her business are, she says, "busier and busier." But this multidimen- sional woman arrived at her success by way of a struggle, in every sense of the word.

When she applied for the position of director of nursing at Meaford General Hospital in 1988, Pat Best felt she was ready for the job. She had worked at St. Andrew's Hospital in Midland since 1971, first as an RN in emergency and the operating room, next as head nurse of the intensive-care unit, and finally as patient care coordinator for the entire hospital. The folks at Meaford apparently agreed, and Best was hired in August with a mandate to balance the nursing budget by the end of the year. In the end she did that, and then some. But the battle to get there was uphill all the way.

"Meaford," she sighs, her wide grin dissolving, "is a very long and difficult story for me." To start, Best lingered in Meaford's shadows, observing for herself how the hospital's nurses operated within the existing structure. Right away, she noted a gurney-full of discrepancies, such as empty wards hosting rosters of unoccupied nurses. When Best inquired, the head nurses told her they "didn't do the schedules." And when she tracked down the person who did, she discovered a tangled and enormously inefficient arrangement whereby none of the full-time nurses was required to work nights or weekends, simply because they preferred not to. Part-time staff were being parachuted in to fill those shifts. All told, this sixty-bed hospital northwest of Toronto, for which the standard formula dictates a nursing staff of 35.8 full-time equivalents, was employing close to 100 nurses.

Best immediately kicked into action, taking over the scheduling duties and insisting that the regular staff pick up night and week-end shifts. Because she deemed some of the nurses in intensive care to be inappropriately trained, she temporarily closed down that unit and sent some of them out for education. Is her administrative style different from how a man might handle the job? Not necessarily, says Best, with some consideration and much twirling of a pen between the fingers. "But I think my personality is what makes me administrate differently. I'm very aggressive. I like to plan things. And I'm difficult to get along with. I'm a perfectionist. I don't back off easily: I set goals and achieve them — regardless. I've had a lot of turnover in staff, probably because of that. It takes a long time for people to understand me, and I may initially come across as being rude — but it isn't so at all."

Between September and the end of that first year, Best's aggressiveness saved the hospital $106,000. But the price of change was a wake of unhappy people, most notably the staff supervisor, who had been unceremoniously ousted from her job as chief scheduler when she'd refused to tackle the modifications Best was demanding. Rumours began to fly through this close-knit hospital in this close-knit town that the newcomer was flexing her muscles and making changes for the sake of change alone. What's more, this upstart had left the community without an intensive care ward and there seemed to be no possible positive motive behind this extreme action. Funding dollars that the hospital was desperately seeking to build a new unit stopped coming in. In their place, angry letters arrived with each mail. And no one ever heard the nursing director's side.

Because it's as important to her story in as many ways as it isn't, it's worth mentioning that Pat Best is black. She was born in Essequibo, a county in Guyana, on November 28, 1941, to a seamstress mother and a father who worked at the ministry of transportation, overseeing workers who built the roads that threaded their part of the country together. But her dad "was into a lot of stuff," including gold fields, and the Hamilton family (Best's maiden name) enjoyed a very comfortable existence. They lived in a vast, servant-catered, green-and-white house across the street from a creek swimming with alligators. In the backyard, a pet buffalo named Rascasa and a passel of pigs ruled.

Best's mother was a determined and resourceful person who stepped into the role of sole caregiver without missing a beat when Pat's father died in 1950. On Sunday, she would convince her three children (Pat has two older brothers, one now a woodworker in Wiarton, Ontario, the other a retired New York police inspector) to attend Sunday school with the promise of homemade ice cream on their return. Today, the memory of somersop-, mango-, and coconut-flavoured coldness lingers for Best, across the miles and the years. When brides and bridesmaids visited her home to be fitted for dresses, Best's mother would forbid them to speak the patois that tumbled out of young people's mouths in Guyana at that time, and insisted that they speak properly. "If people don't speak appropriately, they'll later find it difficult to write appropriately," Best says.

"Because this is the way we were brought up, it's helped me tremendously. I'm grateful for what she did."

Young Pat Hamilton's dolls were always sick and forever the recipients of loving applications of bandages and other salves to heal their varied wounds. Still, this natural caregiver was initially bound for teacher's college, because she excelled at math, and a public school teacher thought she should teach. She may have done so had that teacher not pushed his man's body on her girl's innocence and insisted on a physical expression of gratitude for the interest he'd taken in her future. So Best went to nursing school instead.

She took a complete nursing school course in Georgetown, but when she arrived at Lewisham General in southeast London, England, in 1965 to take a midwifery course ("because England is the absolute best place for training nurses"), they claimed she'd acquired the equivalent of only two years of British nursing requirements. After another year of training there, Best came to Toronto with her husband, James Best, whom she'd married in Guyana, in 1969. She chose not to return to her home country because, she says, "after doing my training, there was nowhere else in Guyana to go."

Best finds nursing exciting and instructive and terribly rewarding. She thrills to see patients recover under her hand, and she gets a tremendous kick from the electric moments of cardiac arrests. One that she'll never forget happened in Midland's St. Andrew's Hospital around 1975. Best was a coronary care nurse in a four-bed intensive care unit there. One night, a woman came flying in the door, pushing her husband in a wheelchair. She headed down the hallway towards the elevators that would take her to emergency in the basement. Best spotted them from across the hall waiting for the elevator and recognized that the man in the chair was in perilous condition. By the time he got to the emergency room, Best thought, he'd be dead. When she said, "Excuse me, can I help you?" the woman explained that her husband was having chest pains. Best swung the chair out of her grip and heaved its occupant onto a bed in the intensive care unit ("I don't know where I got the energy from"). As soon as he landed on the bed, he became unconscious. When she put him on a monitor and saw that he was in a cardiac arrhythmia that was death-producing, Best called a code, got the paddles, and zapped him. He came to. She had no permission to do what she was doing, and the patient hadn't even filled out any paperwork. The team came, they got an IV started, and a few days later, the man walked out of the hospital. Every time the man and his wife see Best, they talk about the experience. "I've saved lots of other lives," Best says, "but this one really stands out."

Other dramas, though, she could live without — like the time she walked into her office at Meaford General one morning to discover her secretary hunched over her desk, crying. When Best inquired, the woman revealed the source of her grief: "I can't take the abuse any more," she sobbed. Best's secretary was buckling under the strain of working for a black woman in a community that would have rather she didn't. Co-workers had sidled past her post and shot out epithets such as "nigger lover" one time too many, and now the secretary had decided to get out of the line of fire. But Best hadn't noticed a thing. She'd been warned about Meaford's small-mindedness before she arrived, and she knew that black people, not so very long ago, had been forbidden to even stop there. She had heeded the advice not to purchase a house in town, choosing instead to settle in nearby Owen Sound. And she'd certainly felt the absence of attention in local stores and watched people step purposefully in front of her in line at the bank. But the hospital itself had always seemed a bit removed from all that, a sanctuary of acceptance in an unaccepting place.

Before she took her leave, Best's secretary suggested she take note of the effect of her arrival in the cafeteria at lunchtime. She did and realized that when she arrived with her tray, nursing staff would leave whether their lunches were eaten or not. She formulated a plan. "I decided they would never eat again." Best spent the next several weeks strategically arriving in the cafeteria just after the lunchtime rush had lifted and as people were settling down to enjoy their meatloaf and fruit cocktail. Best got a lot of enjoyment from the display that followed, as nurses dumped their trays of barely touched food on the conveyor belt and rushed from the cafeteria. "I had some fun," Best recalls, the sparkle back in her eyes.

But fun during this period at Meaford General was mostly in scarce supply for its new director of nursing. An unofficial campaign was launched against her in town, and the locals became increasingly poisoned against her. Then, in June 1989, Best unearthed a shocking incident at the hospital that reeked of incompetence and sent another nurse back to college for retraining. "The administrator who hired me couldn't take any more of it, and he retired," Best explains, and her shoulders quake under her black suit jacket. The tears are still close to the surface, even after the passage of time. "The chairman of the board also quit. Many other board members decided that they were going to leave the board. They were getting harassed in their private lives, and they decided they didn't want to run any more. It was frustrating for them because of how the community responded. The community wanted me fired, but they knew I had done nothing wrong."

On an unseasonably warm morning in May 1990, Best arrived at the hospital at eight o'clock and was greeted by two board members and the new hospital administrator. "Don't sit down," they told her, and the administrator instructed her to come to his office right away. There they explained that there were too many things happening, too many unhappy staff. Her mandate was finished, they said, and it was time for her to move on. The administrator followed Best back to her office and watched her pack books into a box. Under his scrutiny, Best became flustered and left some on the shelves. She loaded her things into her car and was gone by nine. "It was," she says, "the worst day of my life."

A few days later, the administrator visited Best's home with his assistant, a cheque for $48,000 — two years' pay, after tax — and a letter they demanded she sign in which she promised not to sue the hospital. Today, hindsight regularly tugs at Best's shirtsleeves and asks why she signed the agreement. But she was vulnerable, she recalls, and shaken to her very foundation by the sudden turn of events. "I didn't want to leave on my own, because I really enjoyed what I was doing. I'm not a quitter. I face my challenges head on."

Because she had two sons to care for — Séan, then nineteen, and Lerone, then fourteen — Best felt the pressure to find new work very keenly. She and her husband had split up two years before, after he'd lost his job, and that put a serious strain on the relationship. Best feels he was jealous of her for her quick sprint up the administrative ladder. He accused her of sleeping with a doctor. "That still bothers me," she admits. "But that's the way he was brought up. That's the way men are in Guyana." Best's husband started hitting her and abusing her verbally. She put up with the pain for a long time so that her kids would have a father at home. Then one day, when Séan was sixteen, he intervened in a fight between his parents and got caught in the physicality of it. Pat Best vowed to never let that happen again. That's when she took her kids, had a house built in Owen Sound for them without telling James, applied for and won the Meaford job, and left.

When she was dismissed from Meaford, Best didn't know what to tell her sons. "I didn't want them to be hurt, and I didn't want them to think we wouldn't have any money, because they were both very active in hockey. I didn't tell them right away. But after I was home for a few days, I knew it was time. I said, 'I will find a job, don't worry about it. I have a full pay for two years, we're not going to lose the house, you're not going to starve, you can still play hockey. And, before the two years are up, Mommy will have a job.'"

For a while, Best kept her eyes on the classified ads. In June, she applied to a posting at Mount Forest Hospital, which was seeking a director of nursing. She thought she had the job sewn up, until the employers checked her references, her Meaford experience prominent among them. Then another job cropped up, this one for director of nursing in the local nursing home. Again Best was interviewed, and again the hiring team was impressed. They phoned her to tell her she was a likely candidate and that they were just waiting for her references to come back. She didn't hear from them again. "At that point, I realized I would never get another job. I realized I would have to make my own job."

When she was in Meaford, Best had participated in a talk delivered by the ministry of health about the provincial government's restructuring plans, and what they would mean for the future of health-care facilities and community care. "That's what gave me the idea that I should be ready." She considered buying into an existing home health-care agency in Barrie. The plan was for her to open a satellite office in Owen Sound, but the agency administrator refused to open her books to Best, and she decided it wasn't worth the risk. In the meantime, she'd begun researching the Owen Sound market and discovered that the agencies servicing that area relied almost entirely on government work. She recognized an opening for an agency that offered care for people on private health insurance plans who required care above and beyond what OHIP (the Ontario Hospital Insurance Plan) was willing to cover.

On August 7, 1990, within three months of her dismissal from Meaford, Pat Best opened her own business in Owen Sound. Because she had Meaford's guilt money, she could afford to open a 400-square-foot office in town where she hoped to be visible to passers-by. She hired a secretary to work half-days and kicked off the business by offering on-site foot care (mostly for the elderly who can't properly care for ingrown toenails, funguses, callouses, and corns). Best's first contract arrived when she ventured into Participation Lodge, a government agency in nearby Holland Centre that cares for disabled people, to ask if they ever needed help. They did, and they assigned her a contract to care for eighteen people in the community. Best hurried out of her meeting and set about hiring eighteen attendants (she's always done her hiring through a bit of news-paper advertising and a lot of word of mouth — today, she's gratefully drawing from the increasing pool of unemployed institutional nurses). "The contracts started coming in after that."

Her second office, in Orangeville, was launched a year and a half later. And Midland opened in August 1994. For a while, business expanded like a well-performing colostomy bag. Her clients are mainly seniors, along with a handful of chronic and palliative patients. Her services, apart from in-home foot care and paramedical services for insurance companies investigating clients, were largely the same as her competition's. But Best had jumped into a market that was poised to take off in an era of shifting health-care priorities. In 1995, the Séan-Lee Community Nursing Agency had its best year yet, grossing more than $600,000. And then work started to slow down. Businesses were sinking or moving their operations to the United States, and they were taking their employees' insured health-care privileges down with the ship. But then, at precisely the right moment, Ontario's premier stepped in with a rescue plan.

"Mike Harris, God bless his soul," Best marvels. "Everyone hates him except me." Harris inadvertently opened up the market for companies such as Best's by deciding that the agencies that had always monopolized the government market (Victorian Order of Nurses, Saint Elizabeth, and the Red Cross, among them) had been doing work on behalf of the government long enough. Harris identified self-employment in agencies like Best's as a possible solution for all the unemployment within the nursing profession, Best explains. "Previously, someone like me, no matter how hard I tried, how good I was, what my proposal was like, could never get into the market to provide service on behalf of the government." But, as of early 1996, the previously chosen ones started losing their government contracts. And Best is among those companies picking up on those opportunities. In fact, hers was the first outside agency to win a coveted government contract and, a year after the fact, she had scored some $450,000 worth of home-care work in Guelph. "That," she predicts, "is just the beginning."

For now, though, Pat Best takes only a modest salary — $3,000 a month — from the company she heads. She wants to keep the money in the company, she says, to build it up into a comfortable position for when her sons take over. Her hopes for her boys are simple: assertion, aggressiveness, and independence. "And I'd like them to not ever hit a woman, ever, regardless of what the situation is." Regrets are another thing she'd have them avoid, because they tend to hover like a shadow for the rest of one's life. For her, the greatest sadness is the path not taken that would have led a young woman to medical school. Since she was forty-five, Best has wanted to study medicine, confident her skills as a diagnostician ("Better than most doctors and that's the absolute truth") would have delivered her far. But her husband disapproved of that choice and, says Best, wouldn't have been supportive of their family situation if she'd been absent at school.

In the road she ended up taking, Pat Best has typical days that start at eight in the morning and finish twelve hours later. She responds to a pager and a car phone that send her spiralling off towards whichever of her three offices requires her attention at the moment. Being on call doesn't bother her at all, but it does irritate her when a patient she's been called to doesn't realize how sick he is and that he should have been in the hospital days before he called her company. But Best mostly manages now and doesn't spend a lot of time with patients — except occasionally, when her company performs private nursing duties for the Meaford General Hospital. As is customary, the agency performs an assessment of the patient before a nurse is assigned. When Meaford is the destination of one of her staff, the company president herself always draws that duty. "I dress to the hilt and wander around the place, saying hello to all the managers. It makes me feel really good." Best, who hires visible minorities every opportunity she gets because she knows they're "at a disadvantage, the same disadvantage that I have and that my children have," was never scared during the temporary free-fall after Meaford. To her, it was a challenge. "I had to prove something to that community, which I've done."

6 DOING WHAT COMES NATURALLY

YEN FUNG

By Gail Youngberg

Yen Fung is a trim woman in her mid-fifties; her thick black hair shows a very few silver streaks and is cropped in the latest style. Her movements are graceful and energetic, even athletic; she grew up in Weekes, Saskatchewan, a now almost vanished farming hamlet 300 kilometres east of Saskatoon, and still reserves her winter Tuesday afternoons for her regular curling game. On the rink, she opts for recreation, not responsibility, and plays lead, leaving the strategy decisions to the skip.

In business, Yen is the sole proprietor of a set of enterprises that now include a Saskatoon health food store, Mom's Bulk Foods; an organic food store, Organic Plus; a restaurant, Genesis; a gift shop, Mom's Treasure Box; a catering business, Deli Fresh Foods; and her own vegetarian and health food label, Smart Choice Foods. Along the way she has purchased the strip mall that houses some of her enterprises, a warehouse with 7,000 square feet of space, 110 acres of riverbank farmland upstream from Saskatoon on the South Saskatchewan River, residential property south of the city, and a number of houses.

Altogether, deducting the existing mortgages on the mall, the exurban Saskatoon property, and a condo in Nelson, British Columbia, purchased for her son, Mark, who is studying there, she estimates their total value at between two and three million dollars.

She has quietly built up this modest empire in less than a dozen years while attracting very little attention in the local business community. She doesn't have time for that sort of thing, she says. She is more interested in thinking about her next venture.

Yen was born into a busy and prosperous household in China. The family owned a small farm about sixty kilometers from Canton and at the end of the Second World War had constructed a new building to house their dry goods business and their residence. Yen's mother ran the business and also helped her mother-in-law, who was a midwife. They had two maids.

Eight-year-old Yen came to Canada with her younger sister and brother, Jean and Sam, and their mother, Gim Guia Chan, in 1952, to join her father, Tong Woon Mark, who had been working and living in Canada for more than thirty years, with only occasional visits to his family in China. Yen's older brother, Arthur, had arrived in 1950. "Tony" Mark's own father had come to Canada before the turn of the century to work on the railroad, eventually buying a farm in Saskatchewan, yet until 1947 they were prevented by Canadian law from bringing the family to join them.

Life in Weekes was very different from what they had known in China. In the early fifties, rural Saskatchewan still had a pioneer flavour. "We didn't have running water at Weekes," Yen remembers. "We didn't even have a well. We sank a well after we got there." At first they cooked over a woodstove and heated with coal and wood, and relied on their icehouse for refrigeration.

Yen remains an expert with an axe. "Ask Ki U," she laughs, referring to her husband, Ki U Fung, a geographer at the University of Saskatchewan. Professor Fung also came from the Canton area, but grew up and attended university in Hong Kong. "When we first got married, we would go camping. I would do all the splitting of the wood, and I would even amaze him. I still split wood for our fireplace here."

None of the family, except Mr. Mark, spoke English. "Not a word," Yen remembers. "Not even my ABCs.

"But I had fun in school," she says. "We did really well. I was editor of our newspaper. Skipped our high-school curling team, for the girls, played volley ball, was back catcher for our softball team. Whatever there was, we joined."

In ten years, she graduated from Grade 12, and in 1962 left Weekes to go to the University of Saskatchewan in Saskatoon. "All the older generation know the hardship that they've gone through — the racism, not having a good command of the English language — they wanted their kids to really do well. And so our folks have always encouraged all of us to go to university. All four of us went."

Yen was hoping to go into medicine, but she did badly her first year, struggling with a heavy load of sciences and her first time away from home. Sidetracked but not derailed, she switched to humanities, took a year in education, and became a teacher.

After she and Ki U married, Yen enjoyed being home with their children, two daughters, Angela and Michelle, and a son, Mark. But by the time Mark, their youngest, entered Grade 1 in 1981, she had become restless. "I thought, goodness, I have a few good years left, why should I be home just housekeeping and coffeeing with my neighbours, when I could be out making my own money instead of asking for a handout? Sure, we shared and had a joint account, and there really was enough money, if we budgeted carefully. But it was just the thought of being home. I'm capable of doing something else. Why shouldn't I?"

Her brother Sam's pottery supplies business was in trouble, so for two years she helped him. She persuaded her parents to lend him an additional $20,000 and worked in the store with him, bagging and pricing chemicals, and taking some pottery classes. While not taking any salary out of the business, Yen and Ki U borrowed $80,000 to invest in it, and Yen worked with Sam to complete the renovations on a former warehouse he had bought to accommodate his enterprise and two art gallery tenants.

In the meantime, in 1981, they learned that Ki U's parents were being allowed to emigrate to Canada from China. The Fungs bought a "mom-and-pop" business for his parents, a small confectionery that had an apartment above the store, on the west side of Saskatoon. However, the senior Fungs' arrival was delayed until 1982.

Yen took over, scrambling to meet the emergency. "I put the kids in Caswell [an elementary school nearby]. I dropped them off at school and then I went and opened the store and they came home for lunch. The kitchen was upstairs and I couldn't go up and down the stairs because I had to look after the store, so I cooked their lunch on a hotplate. The kids were really good. I'd have to go to the bank, so I would give them their lunch and they would look after the store for me for a few minutes while I dashed to the bank and got my change and all that."

The senior Fungs arrived in May 1982, but illness prevented them from running the store. Yen says now that it was good experience for her, but it was hard work, too. The store is located in a very low-income area, on the edge of Saskatoon's former warehouse district.

"I learned that if you keep the place clean and tidy and provide the stuff that consumers are looking for, they will come. Especially if you give them good service. So I learned to give good service, at the hours that they wanted — which required longer hours. Whatever they wanted, I brought it in. So I had a good customer base there, actually.

"I brought in a few pottery items and I sold a few of those. I made some good friends. The older women that lived around there, they came in and we had coffee and we would chat. To this day I still keep in touch with a couple of them. Mother's Day, you know, I take some tea over and have a good visit with them."

Yen cleared enough to buy the house next door, and then the house next to that. After three years, she accompanied her husband to Somalia on an academic exchange and handed over the operation of the store to a "nephew," Philip Chan, who had just brought his bride over from China and needed employment. Yen explains, "I am his auntie by courtesy in Chinese, because I am of his mother's generation, but in English he is my mother's cousin."

When she got back from Africa, she was going to go into pottery. She took over the house next to the store for her studio and painted it.

"So one day, after finishing the cupboards, I was making myself some tea and looking through the business section in the paper, just to see what was out there, and here a health food store was for sale on 22nd Street. So I went and had a look at it, and I thought, 'Oh, there's some possibilities here.'"

She didn't get any support at home, at first. "Ki U said, 'What for? Just stay home and look after the kids.' I said, 'No, I want to be able to make some money for myself.'"

"My dad always said to me, 'Yen, if you really want to make money you have to go into business for yourself.' Which is true. Because you get to write off all your expenses, and what's left is yours."

Yen's father had proved his point several times over. When he first came to Canada, he did not even have the $500 head tax imposed on Chinese men entering Canada to work. He was obliged to wait thirty days in the "holding pen" in Victoria, British Columbia, while the authorities contacted his father. After working in various enterprises, he formed a partnership with five other men in a similar situation and entered the restaurant business, leaving the partnership when his own family joined him. When his children began going to university, he bought a restaurant in Sutherland, on the outskirts of Saskatoon, where they lived and helped out between classes to help pay their way. Later, he and his wife also moved to Saskatoon and established the Orient Trading Company store.

However, even her brother Sam, who had introduced her to the world of bean sprouts and kelp and eating macrobiotically, and had brought organic foods into their parents' store, was negative.

"He said, 'Yen, what do you know about health food stores?' I really didn't know anything. But I said, 'Well, I'm not exactly dumb. And we've grown up in the business world.'"

Yen persisted. "I went and had another look at it, and looked at their books. And I thought, 'No, it definitely does have possibilities.'" But she had to win over Ki U, because she had no real assets. The store she had so successfully run was in her husband's name.

"It's been interesting. I think women have been resilient. To really work when they see opportunity is there. It took me quite a bit of talking before he came down, because the bank wouldn't lend me the money. I was just a housewife. I needed his signature on the paper. Can you imagine? If I wasn't really strong-willed, I would have said, 'Oh, heck, then I'll just stay home.' I mean, I wouldn't have starved to death. Some women would have said, forget it. But I said, 'No, I see an opportunity here, and it should be taken advantage of.'"

Yen's feelings about the role of women are quietly but deeply held. She remembers seeing abandoned babies on the side of the road on her way to school in China, girl babies whom no one saved.

"You know, there are orphanages in China now, they pick up these girl babies. Couples are only allowed one child. So for women that don't have an abortion and have these children, they abandon them. Out of 400 babies in this orphanage, only one is male, and that's because the male is retarded. Couples keep the boys. Can they imagine how stupid they are? When all these boys grow up, where are they going to find wives to have babies with?"

In the end, Yen prevailed. Ki U did sign the required papers, and in 1985 the Fungs borrowed $100,000 to finance the purchase of the store. They also put in $60,000 of their own money. Yen's new acquisition, Mom's Bulk Foods, was in a small frame building next to a strip mall on 22nd Street, on the west side of the downtown, where the zoning shifts between commercial and residential. Yen kept the name and bought the house next door, hoping that she could eventually tear down the two and build new premises. But the city refused to extend the commercial zoning.

Yen stayed where she was and applied the lessons from the grocery store. In three years, she increased sales from $185,000 annually to $600,000. In 1988, she bought the small neighbouring strip mall and moved her growing business into the mall. Then, when she was extended to the limit, a major tenant in the mall, a restaurant, failed, and she found it almost impossible to find another willing to guarantee the rent.

She decided to launch her own restaurant and called in the earlier loan to Sam. It was a chance to put what she had been learning about macrobiotic and vegetarian cooking to use. But, suspecting that these alone might not carry a restaurant in the Saskatoon market (population 200,000), she obtained a liquor licence and "threw in the Chinese line."

She says, pragmatically, "I think it's the Chinese line that helps the restaurant survive. Purely vegetarian, no. It wouldn't."

Genesis, the "best health food restaurant and Chinese restaurant in Saskatoon," according to the *Globe and Mail*, has done more than survive. It is one of the most popular eateries in the city, with long line-ups for Sunday dim sum. But in the beginning it seemed like the worst decision Yen had ever made.

"You know, I swore when I was a kid, because my folks were always in restaurants and groceries, that I would never do a restaurant. I was up at 7:30 and I stayed until late, coming in and making sure the desserts were done. I lost twenty pounds the first three months.

"And Ki U was on my case. I nearly killed him, actually, because he was so hard on me. Because our house was held as security by the bank, and he was freaking out. 'Calm down,' I said. 'I asked for two years so give me two years.' But you know, it's scary when you borrow that kind of money and plunk it in there."

She was also keeping an eye on Mom's. As it was right next door, the staff there could talk to her if they had any problems. Fortunately, at Mom's she had Irene Puderak, who had been with her since 1985, and Janet Kong, who had come a year later.

"I rely on them totally. As long as they have enough staff, I don't worry about them."

Yen carried on until 1991, until Genesis was a success, and Mom's Bulk Foods was grossing more than $1 million a year. But she was at the end of her tether, and so was her "nephew," Jackie Lu, Ki U's cousin, who had trained in vegetarian cooking in Hong Kong and come over to help with the restaurant. After six months, he wanted out. Fortunately, Philip Chan was willing to take on Genesis. "I switched the boys around, and it worked out really well."

Now, Yen says, "We work on a percentage basis. So I'm getting good money out of it without having to work, which is nice."

One chore Yen kept for herself until recently was to shovel snow off the walks along the storefronts in the mall. "I used to clean all our walks, at Mom's Bulk Foods. I thought, 'No, I'm too old for this,' so this winter I got a guy to do all the walks. But it's exercise. And I got a little bit of fresh air."

The Genesis experience taught Yen to change her style. "I have learned to delegate responsibilities to people and hold them responsible for their portion of it. And to keep in touch with them. Don't leave them hanging there. Talk with them about it, help them with the problem. It they're afraid to move, you're sunk. Go in there and touch base with them, and give them some choices, and let them make the choice."

In the meantime, Mom's was bursting at the seams. In vitamins alone they had gone from a single line to more than half a dozen lines. They provided consulting rooms to a Chinese acupuncture and herbal specialist and were developing the Chinese herb collection, which now contains hundreds of items. Books on nutrition, general health, the environment, and alternative medicine were being brought in. Customers had to inch past one another in the narrow aisles, constantly threatening shelves crowded with organic pastas, wild honeys, dried fruits, and a seemingly endless supply of good things.

One of the mall tenants was moving out, and Yen puzzled over how to use the space. "I didn't know what to move over. I didn't want to split. So I talked to the staff. It's important when you're in business that you take the staff into consideration, let them have their input into it. So that everybody feels like they're part of the picture. They didn't want me to move the books. I asked, 'What can we move out of here that would not cause it to look like it was not a health food store?' Because when people walk in there, they say, 'Wow, you have everything in here.' And they're really impressed. Because we have so much inventory."

They decided to move the body care products over. Ycn added gift items and opened Mom's Treasure Box. "It was like Christmas every day for me, bringing in new things." She went to the trade shows in Canada and overseas, and in China she found some things the trade shows didn't have.

"I want to get into products that would help people to get well, such as magnets, and my 'harmony balls.' There's a magnet in there and there's sort of a tone when you move it. It's very pleasant. Everybody can use it, even invalids, you know, hold it in their hands and turn it around so that it touches the surface of their hands or even the bottom of their feet. So even if they do a little bit of movement five minutes one day and just gently increase it, you know, it helps with the circulation."

In 1993, she moved on to another project, prepared foods and packaged meals under her own label. She bought a former warehouse with 7,000 square feet of space to house the new enterprise, and a small catering company, which her daughter, Michelle, and her husband run. The Fungs and their son-in-law did the renovations themselves, installing a commercial kitchen. She is moving cautiously.

"Right now I'm in the process of redoing my label." Her own label, Smart Choice Foods, has been challenged in Ontario by a company with a similar name. "I've been to a few trade shows, taking my product there. There were people who were interested. We want to export into the United States, and they require a nutritional analysis. So I'm in the process of doing that.

"I'm creating my own recipes. I want organic products, with no additives. I have a couple of products that are really selling well. A vegetarian stew that's a combination of east and west. I love squashes, so that's in it. I love chestnuts, so I have that in there, and I have lotus root in there, which is very good. Carrots. I lean a little bit towards the macrobiotics, so they don't like potatoes, like nightshade vegetables. I'm trying to cater to people who have problems, such as the coeliac people, who cannot tolerate gluten. But vegetarians need a source of protein, so I have some recipes with gluten in them. The Chinese and eastern people, like Japanese, they use quite a bit of gluten as a meat substitute. And it has that texture, as well. You bite into it and it feels like it's meat. Something solid, something to chew on. So that's for people in transition, coming off a meat diet, into vegetarian."

Her market research remains the same — sitting and thinking about it, and talking to people.

She finds that networking through the trade shows and industry seminars works. Few are too competitive to share information. "It depends on yourself. How willing are you to share your information and problems? When you meet on a one-to-one basis, people are generally very open."

She continues to find new directions opening up before her. "If I were bored or something, I think I would call it quits, but I'm still excited. There's so many new things that I could be involved in."

One possibility is the development of a retreat on a small farm north of Saskatoon, with a half-mile frontage on the South Saskatchewan River. She bought the 110-acre property at the height of her stress period with the restaurant. When she talks about it, she clasps her hands together and leans forward.

"A place where people can go and relax, for a week at a time. We show them how to cook properly. Go out and take them on herb walks to see what is out there. You know, we're so tense, we're so involved with our daily things, we don't relax. We have to allow our body to recuperate. And there are so many people who are not well. We want to take them, show them how to exercise properly, show them how to eat properly, get out there, walk the land, breathe the fresh air."

She is also thinking in quite another direction, about an organic supermarket. In 1993, her husband suggested an organic produce store in the original Mom's Bulk Foods property, when the sitting tenant left. Preoccupied with the new catering business and developing her own health food label, she left the project, Organic Plus, largely to him. Now she envisions having everything under one roof. "I think we're ready for it."

She employs more than a dozen people in her various enterprises, not counting the twenty-five staff at Genesis. She can laugh, now, about her early struggles to persuade her husband to support her in her first venture.

"He's resisted. I dragged him into all of this, but, you know, when the money started coming in from Mom's Bulk Foods, he really got excited. He cashes out all my stores. He banks it and keeps tabs on the money. So whenever I go to the bank or need a loan or something, he does all that for me."

Mom's Bulk Foods has been the source of capital for all her subsequent ventures, and Yen remains the sole officer. "I run everything. I work around him. I told him, 'Ki U, I win every time, so why do you give me this?' Well, we can laugh about it. He grounds me. I'm a bit of a dreamer. But you have to dream and make your dreams come true, right? That's what I tell my kids. If you have a dream, work on it.

"Life is interesting. It really is. Each day brings a new experience. Live on a daily basis. Learn on a daily basis."

7 LOOKING GOOD
LISE WATIER

By Rosa Harris-Adler

To many women in Quebec, Lise Watier, fifty-five, is an icon. For more than three decades, the elegant Montrealer, who today heads a cosmetics concern with annual sales of over $15 million and is a member of the Order of Canada, has been the province's premier arbiter of chic. A high-school graduate who studied Latin and philosophy with nuns, she is the only child of a middle-class Montreal family — her father managed a car dealership. But it was her mother, Laurette, who set an unusual example. At a time when the powerful Catholic Church had limited the role of most Quebec women to devotion and procreation, Laurette was a buyer for her sister's clothing store. Laurette's taste, ambition, and success had a visceral influence on Watier, who would visit the manufacturers with her mother and listen intently as they discussed colours and style. When she came of age herself during an era of dramatic social change, she was ready to help shape that change.

Watier began her first career as a television host in 1963, when married women were still legally considered minors in Quebec. Two years later, she was the sole proprietor — and only employee — of her own charm and etiquette school, which first took the form of a Berlitz-style course offered on long-playing records, but which grew to a full-fledged institute by 1968. Then, in 1972, when only 10 percent of working women across Canada owned businesses or served as managers, she began manufacturing and marketing her own line of cosmetics, entering a cut-throat industry with deceptively casual aplomb.

Her venture went on to outlive her first marriage, withstand two brutal recessions, and face down a major catastrophe. With her understated entrepreneurial hustle and keen survival instincts, she epitomizes Quebec's Quiet Revolution, feminist version. Today, she employs 170 people and sells her 300 skin-care, make-up, and perfume products to more than 450 outlets across Canada and abroad. She is a steel *fleur-de-lis*.

Her personal style is evident everywhere throughout l'Institut Lise Watier, her five-storey spa on Laurier Avenue in Outremont, one of Montreal's tonier neighbourhoods. The biggest of its kind in North America, the spa houses a storefront boutique that does a brisk business in the perfumes, lipsticks, potions, blushes, and shadows that are her stock-in-trade. A circular staircase leads to the hair salon, where everywhere walls of mirrors reflect images of women working to make other women beautiful — cutting, styling, curling, dyeing hair. Elsewhere, an army of estheticians with magic fingers performs the arcane arts of facials and massages in small cubicles behind frosted windows and doors.

Watier's own headquarters is located in a more industrial sector of Montreal — off the Decarie Expressway, a noisy, overcrowded thoroughfare, where the racket of traffic competes with the din of planes flying overhead. It is here that she works closely with her core staff of nine. Her right-hand man is Jean-Pierre Guay, the company's managing director, who worked with Watier in the early days, left for a job with Dior, and returned with expanded experience and ideas. "My directors report to my VPs and everyone reports to Jean-Pierre," she explains. "I don't want them reporting to me. I'm too sensitive. But they know I'm there."

So is her family. Marie-Lise, twenty-five, is a lawyer with her mother's enterprise, and another daughter, Nathalie, twenty-two, will join the firm when she graduates from the Université de Montréal's business school. Watier's second husband, Serge Rocheleau, serves as a financial adviser, and her step-daugher, Katerine, is in charge of the spa and exports.

Half of the senior management is made up of women — a factor, says communications director Daphne Tsadilas, that contributes to an atmosphere of quiet harmony. But she adds that the principal reason staffers enjoy coming to work each day is the boss. "There isn't the kind of tension here that you find working in other places," she says, "and a lot has to do with Lise herself. Her calm disposition and gentle mannerisms have become part of the culture here, affecting us all. It's a great team."

As Watier walks through the facilities, she greets many staffers by name and stops to chat about an upcoming birthday celebration. She encounters an energetic young man. They hug, and he tells her how well a group of cosmeticians he's working with is responding to a new line of products. The meeting is warm, intense, and positive.

Her own office is an island of well-appointed sanity, an exercise in textured browns and blacks. Two *faux* leopardskin chairs are welcoming. A large mirror predominates, and books of Renoir and Van Gogh reproductions are scattered about. In one corner stands a huge wooden giraffe, a gift, she will reveal later, from Rocheleau. The smaller giraffe at its side was a present from her staff.

Wearing a striking brown dress accented by the colourful flash of an orange and gold scarf, she's a sophisticated beauty with enormous warm eyes, poreless skin, and honey-coloured hair, perfectly turned out in keeping with the image. She rises at 6:30 each morning, does a half-hour workout on a treadmill at home and heads for the office. She remains there usually until 7 p.m. — a routine she often maintains seven days a week. As she settles in to discuss her life, her big multi-diamonded rings flashing in the light, she speaks in modulated tones that convey her sense of confidence, her inherent and impeccable taste.

"I was attracted to beauty, even in my teens," she says of the career path that led her to be named one of Canada's ten entrepreneurs of the decade by *Profit Magazine* in 1992. "I was always the one to cut the hair and do the make-up for my classmates for a dance, even though I didn't go to the dances much myself. I get it from my mother, who is still a very beautiful woman. From early on, I was enamoured of her grace and panache. Then I read Helena Rubenstein's autobiography, and I discovered what beauty could do. That book traced out the road for me, showed me what I was going to do with my life."

Fate also played a hand. One evening in 1962, when she stopped at a Montreal television station to pick up a friend who worked there, she suddenly found herself being ushered into a studio to do a commercial. ("It was a pure mistake," she recounts now. "They were waiting for someone who hadn't turned up, so I got the job.")

That led to work on various women's magazine-style programs, positions she kept for five years. Throughout it all, she interviewed scores of women and fielded hundreds of questions on beauty and etiquette. It would all prove to be fodder for market research when she launched her successful record series and school. By 1968, she was ready to give up her TV career and devote all her attention to the burgeoning enterprise. She knew her TV work would provide steady income, but she also knew she couldn't count on it and she cherished her independence above all.

"The station could keep me on or let me go at will," she explains. "I had a profound need to be in charge of my own life. I incorporated in 1965 because I already knew where I was going. Even though I was just twenty-two, I had this vision then that took in every activity I'm involved in today." She says starting her own cosmetics company in the seventies was a natural step to making the vision a reality.

It may have been natural for her, but at the time, the decision to launch a manufacturing career was daring for a woman and was met with resistance. "All kinds of people told me I was crazy to try," she says now. "They warned me that the competition was too strong and that I couldn't make it. But maybe I'm still here today because I didn't think about the competition then. I just wanted to deliver quality products."

The basis for the quality products she had in mind was aloe vera, a plant she'd learned of while travelling in Mexico, where women used extracts from the cactus-like shrub as an all-purpose ointment and cosmetic. Impressed with the texture and condition of the skin of these Mexican women, Watier decided to import the substance for use in products she planned to develop.

Back in Montreal, Watier did her legwork and found a sympathetic chemist who specialized in cosmetics. "He was a very old and patient man," Watier recalls. "My only knowledge of chemistry is what I'd learned at school. But he took the time to teach me what combination of ingredients would work together and to help me create products that were unique. I'll never be a chemist, although I've worked with many since that time and I've come to understand a lot about formulas. But he gave me that solid grounding."

With no business training and little cash on hand, she operated on instinct, naïveté, and her powerful conviction that she understood the hearts and souls of her potential clientele. "The best thing I had going for me was my knowledge of women," she says. "I certainly didn't have much money — just what I had built up with my first business. But I had respect in the marketplace I was entering — and that was better than a business degree."

She did have the support of her then husband, Guillermo Andrade, whom she had married in 1970. Together with Andrade, a business-school graduate with some experience as a hotel manager in Acapulco, she handled the administrative details while staying focused on the big picture. It was Watier alone, however, who chose the colours, fragrances, and themes that would make or break her. She began travelling to Europe, making contacts in the fashion community and keeping her eye on colour trends that would influence North American women in a year's time. "But even some of the most fashionable colours, like it or not, are just not very flattering," she says, so she used her own sense of creativity and taste to determine which colours to select for her line.

By contrast, it was her practical side that prevented the company from becoming too big, too fast. She avoided borrowing in the early years, instead preferring to keep her product lines modest and her output small. "I started slowly," she elaborates. "I never spent more than I had. I didn't buy 3,000 jars the first time I worked with my chemist. I asked him: 'How small a batch can you make?' He told me 144 jars. So I said: 'Could you give me half that amount?' And he said he would if he could keep the rest. That's how it began. My initial plan was to conquer the world, but in reality, the world is not an easy place to conquer. I learned through the years that I had to build step by step, solidly. I didn't go crazy. It took me a long time before I went to see the banks for a loan."

When her cosmetics enterprise was new, Watier learned the art of the pitch. With little money to put into advertising, she understood that to bring her products to market she'd have to sell to the big retail chains door-to-door, trading on her TV celebrity status. In 1972, she approached Clayre Clément, then a cosmetics manager for a Sears outlet in Quebec. Familiar with Watier from her TV appearances, Clément says she was impressed by the courage of this Québécoise woman who dared compete with Estée Lauder. She took a chance and let Watier give her her best shot. It persuaded her to try her product line — her first big break. Still, even as her products began to sell steadily, she limited her marketplace exposure, a savvy strategy meant to enhance the prestige image of her line.

Over the next eighteen years, Watier's products gained a modest toehold in the $1.6-billion Canadian cosmetics industry. Drawn by word of mouth and Watier's star status, consumers stayed with the products because they were priced well for their quality and were on the cutting edge of fashion without being too *outré*. In Quebec, they were best-sellers: by the mid-1980s her wares were outperforming all other brands everywhere but in downtown Montreal, where department stores still promoted more established companies. Always aware of the importance of being *à la mode* in her trade, Watier was constantly renewing product packaging, make-up shades, and perfume lines, keeping a careful eye on quality control. She said, at the time, that she had to be "faster, better, smarter, and nicer" to compete with cosmetics giants with money to burn on advertising.

Along the way, Watier had Marie-Lise and Nathalie. When they were infants, she'd bring them to the office when she could, but leaving them was hell when she had to travel to Europe to check out make-up trends and to meet with suppliers.

"I'd be miserable on the plane. I'd cry for hours," she says of those days. "Motherhood was always more important to me than business. I'm a mother hen and I loved fussing over my children. But I had very good help I could rely on for many years. I suppose being somewhat on their own gave my children a sense of responsibility. They became strong. And because so much of my energy was devoted to business, they learned to participate. I would share things all the time with them over breakfast and dinner. They became involved in every aspect of my work when they were very young."

Watier's marriage to Andrade, however, was foundering by the early eighties. Andrade, then president of Lise Watier, has said in interviews that Watier "felt that she was number two" and that she wrongly believed she didn't get sufficient credit for her work. He has said that she downplayed his own role, adding that the couple's power struggle helped bring the marriage to an end in 1983. Although Watier acknowledges Andrade's contribution to the firm, she remains reluctant to talk about her personal life.

Despite the trouble at home, the company kept growing — and with success came the need to catch the wave and explore the potential for further development. The booming economy of the late eighties translated into a strong upward curve in sales, and Watier began to look towards the international marketplace. For the first time, Watier needed other people's money to keep up with the demand for her products and to move forward. She established a line of credit at her bank. Because of her track record, the lenders welcomed her.

"With time and growth, you have to make plans, expand — and you need more money to do it," she says now in hindsight. "So you go to the banks. Suddenly, you have access to money and maybe you spend more than you should because you can. Sometimes the risks you take are good, sometimes they're not. But you do it because you have to plunge in. And you learn."

What she learned, among other things, was that bankers can be fair-weather friends. In 1990, just as the economy began experiencing its worst crash since the Depression, a flash fire reduced Watier's headquarters to cinders. Insurance helped, but she had no products to deliver in a stalled business environment where demand had plummeted anyway. Times were grim.

"To see twenty years of your life totally destroyed, burned down to the ground..." There is a pause as she collects herself. "I didn't even hesitate. I don't actually remember the next morning, but people tell me I literally rolled up my sleeves and said, 'We're starting over.' I don't know where I got the energy, but we began again."

Before the fire, Watier had committed to bringing her products to a wider national market. In anticipation, she repackaged the line and began charging slightly more for her goods, which had always been priced moderately to appeal to women who wanted something better than dime-store products but less high-end than Dior. Consumers didn't respond well to the price hike and, as the recession became entrenched, sales dropped precariously.

"We lost a lot of money in that era," she says, "because even though my costs and my standards stayed high, I had to lower my prices. I refused to skimp on quality. Soon, the banks were after me. Some of them were around me like sharks, nipping at me all the time. Ironically, some of those sharks were women. Maybe they were jealous or felt they had something to prove — I don't know. But I refused to give them the scent of my blood."

She says she knocked on "at least 100 doors" looking for financial support, but bankers who'd been eager to help in the past gave her the cold shoulder.

"There were times when I wasn't sure I could make payroll, and the thought of not being able to write a cheque for my employees was very, very hard," she recalls. "In a way, it kept me going. I had a huge responsibility to the women who had worked with me for so many years. They believed in me. They believed in opportunity for women because of me. I'm a pioneer in Quebec. I would have disappointed so many if I'd given up. So even when all my financial advisers were telling me to close down, I wouldn't do it. If you give up, you have no hope of a solution, but as long as you have faith, you can find one."

Finally, a financial angel stepped in, she says, but in keeping with her private nature, she won't reveal who. "All I'll say is that at the very last moment, I was saved," she elaborates. "The sharks never believed I had it in me."

Rebuilding was difficult, but the staff hung in. "Some people have been with me for twenty-five years," says Watier. "My team here is generally young and they share my passion and ambition. We're all believers and that's what kept us going through extremely trying times."

By November 1993, a successful turnaround hinged on the launch of Watier's new fragrance, Neiges. Characteristically, she stuck with the name (which translates as "snow") despite the protests of those around her. "My husband, my family, they all said, '*Neiges!* Ugh! Cold! We hate it!'" she recalls now, laughing. "But I said, 'You're forgetting something. *Neiges* is purity. When I was a child I saw snow as magical, and even today when I see it coming down it represents to me refinement. I know my clientele. So I took the risk. I wanted a fragrance that was light and enduring, that would make a statement worldwide, that would project Canadian women, and I found it." Today Neiges, the top-selling fragrance in Quebec and doing brisk business in Bay and Sears stores across Canada, has shown remarkable staying power and momentum.

"It's been a true phenomenon," she says now. "Usually the second year after a fragrance hits the market, there's a plateau and then sales drop. But after the fourth Christmas, sales of Neiges are still climbing. So of course the companies who used to be number one are wondering what's up. Its success gave me and all my employees back our sense of pride, especially coming at that time, after the fire, after the sharks. It made all of us feel 'Yes! We did something very well!'"

Now, Neiges and other Watier products are sold in France, the Middle East, and Taiwan — her first foothold in Asia.

In retrospect, she says she entered a tough industry — but one where her gender proved an advantage. "I never was made to feel inferior by either my suppliers, my clients, or my customers," she maintains. "Everyone understands I've given my life to women and I know what I'm talking about. I use these products — I'm close to them. Of course, a few individuals along the way made me aware of my gender. But I'm convinced commitment is more important than gender or anything else. To make it in any business, it's not enough to give 100 percent. If that's all you have in you, go work for someone else and give *them* 100 percent. You have to give 200 percent. That's how it happens. That's what pulls you through."

8 CATERING TO SUCCESS
GAIL HALL

By Liane Faulder

Chaos rules, and the guests are due to arrive in less than an hour. Bright-red gerbera daisies and swaths of fat pussy willows are strewn on the carpeted floor of the reception area. The serving tables are empty. An extension cord is missing, coffee has yet to perk, and one of the servers has a nosebleed.

But Gail Hall, owner of Gourmet Goodies, one of Edmonton's largest caterers and arguably its most prestigious, charges through the scene with surprising good cheer. She's getting by on just a couple of hours of sleep — "I've got this insomnia thing happening" — and ahead of her stretches another reception and a good twelve hours of hard slogging.

"Honest, I feel great," says Hall, as she unpacks a box of tiny red and gold tea cups, accessories for an Asian buffet for 200 she's pulling together with seven of her staff to mark the opening of Ghengis Khan, a rare exhibit of Mongolian artifacts at the Provincial Museum of Alberta. "I like setting up. The adrenaline rush is incredible. Other parts of small business I find difficult, but 'doing' is good therapy for me."

By the time guests trickle in, heavy-duty "doing" has resulted in a polished opulence complete with rice-paper screens and Asian art. Sparkling glass plates of spring rolls with bowls of hot and spicy dipping sauce are arranged at the perfect angle among tall black vases of red gladioli and ginger flowers. Woven baskets of *fat bao* — Chinese buns — nestle next to the hot dishes, including delicately flavoured green onion cake and sliced pork tenderloin.

Hall has slipped out of her Gourmet Goodies T-shirt and into a black brocade, mandarin-style jacket to observe the event with the earnest, attentive air of someone who fusses. She listens for the sound of guests oohing and aahing over the Chinese noodle salad, watches for the telltale lips pursed with pleasure.

"This business gives me what I need to live," Hall says of Gourmet Goodies, and she's referring to more than food or income. "I need to know people like me and the food I do. Feeding people gives me a kind of instant reward that's really important to me."

Hall has been working on that so-called "instant reward" for more than ten years, building Gourmet Goodies from a one-woman show to a business with sixty-three employees and which brought in $1.2 million in sales in 1996. The firm, specializing in tailor-made occasions for two or two hundred, is a nearly perfect reflection of Hall — her background, passions, and insecurities.

Gourmet Goodies began officially in the mid-eighties. That's when Hall, acting on a push from her husband, Jon, quit a government job — giving up more than half the family income to pursue a catering career.

The roots of the business go deeper still, back to a pickle factory in suburban Toronto — one of a series of small businesses owned by Hall's father, Soll Silverberg. "I remember being about eight and standing in a vat in sterilized boots, like hip-waders, grinding pickles into relish at the factory and having a great time," Hall recalls with fondness.

Her parents, both Polish immigrants, worked hard in the family operations, which ranged from a small coffee shop to a company that made footstools. Gail had a lot of responsibility around the house at an early age; she was rolling out knishes and blintzes for her mother, Frances, by the time she was seven. "The one way I got attention at home was by preparing food and having people tell me it was good."

Until she was in her early thirties, Gail's devotion to food was no more than a hobby. "I loved food, I gave great dinner parties, but I never thought I could make a living doing something I loved," says Hall, who spent her twenties pursuing a sociology degree and establishing herself in the field of refugee settlement.

In 1981, while attending a conference in Ottawa, Gail met her husband-to-be, a business consultant from Edmonton. The two clicked instantly, and after conducting a cross-country courtship, they married in 1982. By that time, Gail had moved west, taking a job as a consultant with the Alberta government's settlement services department. But she wasn't happy working within a bureaucracy. "I never got to see the end results of my work," she says.

Exhibiting his characteristic talent for envisioning the future, Jon bought Gail a book called *Cash from Your Kitchen* and treated her to a week at Vancouver's Pierre Dubrielle cooking school as an anniversary gift. "It was a wonderful week and it really reinforced for me how much I loved food and cooking," says Hall, a no-baloney sort of woman whose day-to-day wear includes comfortable corduroy pants and sensible shoes. "I realized I was instinctively good at this. It was a turning point for me."

Still, it took a couple of years for Hall to prepare mentally for a change, and even then, she spent six months doing research on catering. She discovered that although lots of Edmonton caterers would do cabbage rolls and perogies for 300, there was nobody who would do a romantic picnic lunch or something other than cold cuts for a business lunch.

"Customizing was the philosophy upon which Gourmet Goodies was born," says Hall. In 1986, with $6,000 cobbled together from her and Jon's savings and a $1,000 loan from her father, Hall got started. The health board decreed she could not work from home without major renovations. So she hauled great bags of groceries to every client's home or office, where she did the food preparation and cooking.

By the fall of 1987, word of mouth and many cold calls had pushed business to roughly $24,000 a year. Hall still wasn't taking in a salary but had hired one part-time person. Cooking out of the clients' place was getting awkward, so Gail leased 1,450 square feet of industrial space for $700 a month in a former chocolate factory, furnished with three used gas stoves and three fridges bought for a total of $300.

Shortly thereafter, although she was already putting in her trademark twelve-hour days, Hall began teaching Gourmet Goodies cooking classes, which continue today. "Sometimes there were classes in which I handed out recipes I hadn't tested till half an hour before the students arrived, but it always worked."

In the next two years, things exploded. "It was before the recession of the early nineties and people were still spending money," recalls Hall. "Corporate work was really on the rise." In 1990, with twelve staff, it was time for more space. Two units of equal size opened up right next to Hall's existing location, so she went to the bank to borrow the $35,000 necessary to install a hot and cold kitchen and a pastry-preparation area.

"Even though we were debt-free and bringing in $350,000 a year, the bank manager, who was a man, wouldn't even look me in the eye. Just gave me a cash-flow projection to fill out," says Hall with disgust. Put off by his lack of support, she found herself a female bank manager who quickly endorsed the loan.

Hall is doubtless a good-news story — the business is debt-free, and she brings in a $21,600 annual salary ($30,000 if you include her company-leased car). She's a caring and attentive boss whose conciliatory, feminine management style is popular with staff. Hall offers dental and medical benefits to employees, as well as a yearly Christmas bonus in an industry famous for poor treatment of workers. She has won numerous awards in the Edmonton business community, including the YWCA's Woman of Distinction award.

"But she refuses to accept she's a success," says Jon, shaking his head in frustration when we talk one night in the cozy, fire-lit living room of the modest Hall home. Her father's business experience — all his companies ultimately failed and the family home was lost to creditors — have left Gail with a profound fear of failure. "Even though I have a proven track record, every day I worry about something going wrong," admits Hall as, ever the caterer, she pours tea and offers Gourmet Goodies white chocolate and oatmeal cookies.

She jokes about needing therapy to cope, and it's true Hall sees a counsellor occasionally to understand why the business keeps her awake nights. Change bothers her, a foible she puts down to the chaotic ups and downs in her childhood home associated with her father's business. "In business, you have to change or you stagnate," says Gail. "But sometimes I think, 'Why can't the world just stop and leave me alone?'"

Luckily, Jon — who holds 49 percent of Gourmet Goodies' shares — has a talent for understanding where Gourmet Goodies needs to go. Though Gail is the boss, Jon consistently encourages her to look to where she wants to be in five years, ten years, and at retirement. He's the force behind Gourmet Goodies' latest venture — cooking tours to exotic locations such as Sante Fe, New Mexico, which Jon sees as a way to imprint Gourmet Goodies as a trendsetter.

The upside of Soll's legacy is that it made Gail a conservative manager who has no other business investments besides Gourmet Goodies, pays cash for most everything, and manages to tuck away a 10 percent yearly profit, which is slightly better than the industry average. She's also grateful to her father for something else. "My dad got into careers he didn't have the training for, but he had the passion," she says, adding that the same blind enthusiasm has got her through many an eighteen-hour day.

The demands of the business mean few personal indulgences for Hall, though she makes time for the odd massage, regular workouts at the gym, and professional voice lessons. She and Jon camp several weeks a year in their 1976 Westfalia van. "I'm happy and healthy. I don't need much," says Hall, with a warm smile.

Her long-term dreams remain rooted in the business — she and Jon are planning a retail face for Gourmet Goodies. She is squirrelling away $2,000 a month from the business so she can approach the bank with 10 percent down on a $600,000 plan to purchase a building within the next several years. "I've spent some $300,000 in rent over the years and that's very motivating," Hall says.

She dreams of a storefront operation with a reception hall on site, a warm, friendly place where customers would be greeted with the scent of fresh bread as they walked in to buy anything from a stir-fry for supper to a range of frozen prepared foods. She knows such an expansion will mean an early retirement is not likely in the cards. And that's okay.

"Sometimes I wonder what I'd do if I was rich and didn't have to work," she speculates. "I'd be bored to death."

9 BUTTERING UP
THE COUNTRY
DOLORES TOBIN

By Kathryn Welbourn

GREG LOCKE

In the early 1900s, a dwarf slowly paced the beach at Cuslett, Newfoundland, about 200 kilometres southwest of St. John's. Little Tom, as he was known, searched through the tangle of tide-tossed debris for decent bits of wood. In those times everyone was expected to have a trade, and Tom was much too small to go fishing — his feet dangled above the floor when he sat on a chair. Tom made his living by carving useful things like walking sticks and print blocks to decorate and mould homemade butter. Tom's work was skilful, even artistic, and it was made to last.

Almost 100 years later and a little farther up the shore, Dolores Tobin likes to tell the tale of Little Tom for several reasons: It's a good story — always worthwhile in the Tobin household — and she admires Tom's craftsmanship and his resourcefulness. As well, Dolores is the proud owner of one of Tom's surviving butter prints. She used the stylized flower carved into a softwood block to make an impression in her butter when she first started to produce and sell her now provincially famous Spyglass Home Style Butter. "He did an unbelievable job on it," she says with admiration. "He had nothing but an old pocket knife to work with."

Ingenuity is something Dolores appreciates. In only seven years, the forty-six-year-old mother of three — Mark, twenty-six, Eddy, twenty-five, and Tim, eighteen — has gone from beating together a few pounds of butter in her kitchen with a wooden spoon, to managing a $300,000-a-year manufacturing operation that supplies a weekly average of 8,000 to 12,000 pounds of her creamy one-pound blocks to major grocery stores across Newfoundland, Nova Scotia, New Brunswick, and the French island of St. Pierre. She employs Mark to run the huge electric churns, and she has two full-time male staff to help with the physical labour. Dolores didn't start making butter to become rich, or because she has always dreamed of owning her own business. Even now she wouldn't call herself an entrepreneur. Like Tom and his carving, the whole point of her business is to make a living, with what she has, right where she lives.

"It would have been a lot simpler if we set up in St. John's," she says, struggling to explain her need to stay in rural Newfoundland. "See, I don't think I'd be able to take to living in a big city. I go to St. John's to visit my customers, I get a headache, I can't wait to get home. The butter is just a way of staying here."

"Here" is her farm in Ship Cove an hour and a half's drive from St. John's along the Trans-Canada Highway and then south past Placentia on Route 100. Population: the Tobin family.

Dolores and her husband, Stan, aren't exactly reclusive. They just need lots of space — away from the world and even away from each other. For example, Stan likes to walk the beach while Dolores prefers the old road in back. "I'm not a beachy person," she says, shaking her head and grinning. "Stan and I are that different. We can't work together. We'd kill each other." Stan doesn't disagree. He calls himself a naturalist and a dreamer who can't stand to know what he's going to do every day. He likes to create and organize a project and then move on, not run it. Stan makes his living by breeding cattle and as a consultant for the Newfoundland and Labrador Environmental Association. He brings his money home in chunks. Dolores is the opposite. She likes to see something concrete at the end of her day. She's got physical strength and a head for business, and she's stubborn. If she says she's going to do something, you can count on it. Dolores makes the steady money in the family, a salary of $600 a week, which is all she can afford to pay herself right now. The Tobins' common ground is their love for the isolation and beauty of Ship Cove. They are completely devoted to the place.

Driving into Ship Cove is the kind of happy chance travellers remember and talk about years later. Divided from Placentia by about twenty miles of grey scrub, jagged beach, and the odd stray ram, its meadows roll open between two steep hills and a twist of treacherous road. Clean streams cut through the fields and woodland fences in the back. A long curve of ocean washes along the front. The Tobins' little bungalow is perched on the southern hill overlooking Stan's small herd of Highland cattle, sturdy, independent little beasts that don't need much care. "The lazy man's cattle," Stan calls them. There are a few outbuildings, a two-storey saltbox, and Dolores's new creamery — a small, clean-looking structure tucked into the hill on the north side.

In Newfoundland, property is not divided into neat square sections, especially cleared land, which is hard to come by. Every corner, scrap, and ridge has been, or will be, divided up among family members. The Tobins' farm is no exception. It's a rough collection of properties accumulated over time, about eight square kilometers. Stan describes Ship Cove as a place full of tranquil nooks and small enchanted places. Dolores calls it a good place to think and a good place to work. You can find her there every day of the week, a fresh-looking woman whose sensible work clothes are offset by a pair of very saucy eyes. Dolores has lived in Ship Cove since she married Stan in 1968 and she never wants to live anywhere else.

Stan is the fourth generation of Tobin men to bring his new bride home to Ship Cove. Even so, tradition had very little to do with Dolores's decision to move into her father-in-law's old house and join the eight other families who made up the community at that time. She was born and raised in Branch, another small outport about 100 kilometres to the southeast, so she knew she'd like the rural life. In fact, a love of the outdoors is what attracted the young Dolores O'Rourke to Stan Tobin in the first place. "We'd walk and hike. We kept company like that for a couple of years and then we got married," she explains. But the reason Dolores agreed to move in to Stan's home community was her desire to work. She had been trained as a nurse in St. John's, and Ship Cove was within driving distance of the cottage hospital in Placentia. "Stan said to me, 'Let's go to Ship Cove for the winter and if you're not contented then, you know, to hell with it,'" Dolores remembers. "I was the first woman to settle there in seventy years, to settle there and stay."

Dolores got her wish. She worked at the hospital for about eighteen years before quitting in order to spend more time with her growing family. "Well, part of it was I got tired of it [nursing] and the other part I suppose was the boys," she says. "When they started getting up in the higher grades they didn't want to study their books or do their lessons or anything, so I thought me staying home would keep on top of things." By then the population of Ship Cove had dwindled to just Dolores's little family and her mother-in-law. "You had to be a digger to stay," Dolores explains. "They married, or moved out for work. The older people died. It just faded away."

This is the last year the school bus will stop in Ship Cove. Dolores's youngest son, Tim, is graduating from high school and plans to go to university. Eddy, her middle child, has already moved out to attend college. It's been fifteen years since anyone except the Tobins lived in the community. And that's the way they like it. It's one of the reasons they stayed. Stan hasn't exactly run people off the place with a shotgun, but he doesn't encourage anyone new to move in. In fact, his current project is to get the area surrounding their farm designated as a nature reserve. On the odd occasion that she does feels a bit lonely, Dolores drives to Placentia or back to Branch to visit relatives. But that doesn't happen very often. Dolores loves the quiet and is happy just walking, bird-watching, or feeding the cattle by herself or with her family.

With her career in nursing at an end and their community practically deserted, Dolores had to find another source of income. She and Stan tried a number of things, including a custom-kill sheep operation supplying fresh carcasses to the major grocery chains on the island. They kept some 250 sheep on the farm and learned how to prepare the meat for sale. "We had a man come in here to show us what to do," she says. "Stan killed them and I cleaned them and took off their skin." But lynx in the area killed all the lambs, and the Tobins had to give it up. "We couldn't really stop them [the lynx]. They were here ahead of us," Dolores says with a laugh. "We lost our shirts at that."

Dolores started making butter soon after that, in 1990. Lynx don't chase cattle, so the small herd of six Jersey cows she had recently purchased were still providing the family with milk. "I just started doing it on the side for money for me, that's all," says Dolores. "I made it by hand in my kitchen and sold it around to friends." She makes it sound simple, but a few pounds of homemade butter can take a couple of days to prepare. Dolores milked the cows, carried home the milk, pasteurized it, and then left it to cool. After that, she would pour it into a hand-turned separator to extract the cream from the milk. She left the cream to sit in a cool place for about twenty-four hours. Next Dolores would "churn" the butter. This meant beating and stirring with a wooden spoon for at least forty-five minutes until the cream turned into butter, and the butter "broke" into small, solid balls. The buttermilk was drained, and the butter balls were washed in cold water in the sink — three times. After the water was drained, Dolores added the salt by hand and worked it through the butter. Then she made her little "prints" using a round mould. It was quite a bit of work for a few pounds of butter.

Hard work has always been a way of life for Dolores. As the oldest of ten children growing up in Branch, a place that didn't have electricity until the late 1960s, she was expected to help her parents. She chopped firewood; worked in the garden; raked the hayfields; tended their few cows, sheep, and hens; and watched the younger children when her mother was out in the fields. That's the way it was when she was a girl, and her memories of that time are happy and full of humour.

"One time when I was about ten, she [Dolores's mother] said, 'Go and look after the baby, but don't pick her up. If you need me, just wave a diaper out the window and I'll come right in.'" Dolores laughs at the memory.

It was during her childhood that Dolores learned to make butter. Her aunt Annie English taught her. "She didn't have any children of her own, and I used to go over there and spend time with her," says Dolores, adding that as a teenager she wasn't always thrilled when her aunt asked her to help make butter. "When you're that age, you want to be out playing with everybody and chasing the boys, and of course I couldn't do that because she wanted me to make butter with her." Dolores recalls the long hours she spent lugging cream and water up to her aunt's parlour. "It was a really nice room, with a chesterfield and drapes and everything. No one was allowed to sit on that chesterfield and still she made her butter in there. It was only the other night that I thought about it — she had her churn and her milk separator set up in there because it was cool."

Aunt Annie was a born businesswoman, just like Dolores. They even looked alike. Annie English sold her butter to the Americans stationed at the military base in Argentia. The well-paid military staff would drive almost 100 kilometres to Branch to get it — and they paid $8 a pound for this luxury in the 1960s. "Her husband was a fisherman, and this is what she would do for her money," says Dolores, adding she didn't need a recipe when she started making butter herself. She had done it so many times with her aunt that she just made it from memory.

But it wasn't until Bidgood's — a supermarket specializing in Newfoundland food — called looking for some of her butter that Dolores realized she might have found the money-maker she was looking for. "I don't know how they found out about it," she says, explaining that the general manager, Helen Bidgood, wanted twenty or thirty pounds of butter right away. Luckily, Stan had brought home a small five-pound electric churn he'd been given as part of a trade for a tractor. "That was still two or three days' work for me. But I got her that and then she called again. It was a novelty. No one else was doing it, so we knew we had a market there."

Helen Bidgood was happy to give Dolores her start in the butter business. "She's worked really hard and been persistent," says Helen, who discovered Dolores's butter through word of mouth. Bidgood's is a family-run business that prides itself on supporting Newfoundland producers. Helen continues to stock Dolores's old-fashioned handmade butter prints. They make the kind of traditional Newfoundland centrepiece her customers love to display at their Sunday dinners. "Dolores had a lot to learn about the regulations and process of the food industry," says Helen. "I helped her out where I could."

Always ready to jump right in, Dolores decided to expand. She needed a marketing consultant, and Stan recommended an acquaintance, Bill Sterling. Dolores hired Bill, who is also the town planner for the city of Corner Brook, at $500 a day to develop a marketing and feasibility study, and then she approached the Atlantic Canada Opportunities Agency (ACOA), a federal government funding organization whose mandate is to assist small and medium-sized businesses. "Bill did an excellent job on the study. ACOA told me their decision was based on how good his work was," she says. ACOA loaned Dolores $26,000, which she had to match with some money of her own. She got the cash by selling her 1956 Pontiac. "That was an antique, really, anyway," she says. "I had another car." Dolores used the money to convert the old abattoir they'd used for slaughtering sheep into a small manufacturing plant. This was the first step in a plan Dolores was determined to follow through on. With the exception of expanding into individual butter patties, the development of her business has gone pretty much as planned.

Dolores's next move was to hire a St. John's welding company, D F Barnes Limited, to make her a new churn. "We were a couple of months at that," she says, laughing. Dolores wanted a churn that could produce thirty to forty pounds of butter at one time. There was no model to work with, so Dolores would pick up some cream at Central Dairies, a large domestic dairy in St. John's, drive down to Barnes, and throw the cream into the new churn to see if it worked. It took a little bit of experimenting to figure out the speed — too slow and nothing would happen; too fast and you've got whipped cream.

"They'd say to me, 'What's wrong with it?' and I'd say, 'I don't know what's wrong with it. It's still not moving fast enough,'" Dolores says, remembering the group of oil-covered welders standing around the churn and staring down in dismay at the snow-white cream. "Well, we finally fixed that all up. We could make 120 pounds a day for five days. We thought we had our fortune made then."

Even with the new churn, Dolores still had to do some jobs by hand: pour in the cream, take it out, and wash the butter. And she still had to package and stamp the butter herself. Dolores hired two full-time staff at $8 an hour — almost double the provincial minimum wage — to help her with the physical labour. "And I'd pay them more than that if I could afford to. They certainly deserve it," she says of the local men she found by asking around in nearby communities. "They just staggered in," she jokes.

Dolores took care of the marketing and distribution herself. She started by making appointments with the managers of grocery stores and delicatessens and then visited them to show off her butter, which she carted around in sixty-pound coolers. "And do you know what I was getting for a pound of butter at that time?" she asks incredulously. "Ten bucks. But we started to make lots of it and the price went down. We flooded our own market," she says, explaining she still gets about $4.50 a pound for her hand-poured prints and $2.60 for her one-pound blocks. "I don't believe in just calling," adds Dolores, who at least once a year visits every store she sells her butter to across the island. "That's the most important thing you can do. Let them put a face to the product. Let them know you and your product are out there." This strategy has worked for Dolores, who built up her clientele until all the major grocery chains in the province were stocking her butter.

Dolores's Jersey cows weren't able to supply her new operation with enough cream. The increased production also meant she had to meet new guidelines for pasteurization, so she hooked up with Central Dairies, buying the company's pasteurized cream and selling it back to them as butter for $2.60 a pound. Dolores says it was a good deal for both companies. Central Dairies had excess pasteurized cream and was looking for a way to utilize it, and Dolores was having a hard time keeping up with her distribution. As part of the deal, Central Dairies began delivering the cream to Ship Cove and picking up the finished butter for distribution, which the company took over. Central Dairies also helped with the marketing, although Dolores continued to make personal contact with all her customers. By 1992, she had produced another market study and applied for more loans to expand her business into completely mechanized production.

Getting funding isn't an easy task, even if you've proven your business can work. "As far as small business on this island, the banks are dead. They didn't help me at all, wouldn't look at me," Dolores says in disgust, and then turns her ire on another organization she finds offensive. In 1992, Enterprise Newfoundland and Labrador was a provincial government agency set up to help small business. ENL was disbanded in late 1996 and has been replaced by the Department of Development and Rural Renewal. But when Dolores applied to ENL, it was still in operation. "I can't stand them and I've got no time for them," she says hotly. When she approached ENL with her business plan, she had carefully priced the equipment she needed. But she says ENL started calling around checking her suppliers — and the price "skyrocketed" when companies found out government funding might be involved. "They nitpicked my plan to death," says Dolores, who became even angrier when ENL started fiddling with her creamery design. "I had it all planned out in my head. The whole layout was designed to be the most convenient and the quickest for me and my staff. They started saying you don't need this and you don't need that, and they didn't know anything about it. When they started fooling with that, I said, forget it, get your hands off my proposal."

Dolores went back to ACOA and secured a $100,000 loan, which she matched by finally selling off her sheep and by borrowing from the Federal Business Development Bank (FBDB).

"I found they were really good. Of course, their interest rates are high, around 18 or 19 percent, and I don't know what they'd be like if you didn't pay your instalments," Dolores says. She calls FBDB the bank of last resort.

She used the loans to build her new creamery and to purchase a larger churn and a printing machine. There were a few problems and more than a few ruined pounds of butter as she learned to use her new equipment, especially the printing machine. But Dolores has slowly worked out the kinks and continues to build up her business. It will take her another eight to ten years to pay off her loans. In the meantime, she has plans. Her creamery could produce 20,000 pounds of butter a week if she had the customers. She is currently expanding into grocery stores in Ontario, has a new contract to supply a St. John's hotel with her original handmade stamps of butter, and is even eyeing the U.S market. "If it could be sold all over Canada in the next ten years, or North America, that would be reasonable."

You might think running a small business would interfere with family life. But Dolores maintains it is possible to look after both. "I just work around it," she says. "I still come home and cook supper. I still bake my homemade bread and do all the washing and the cleaning. I'm one of those people that enjoy getting up early in the morning and doing whatever needs to be done."

Dolores says her strength comes from her desire to stay in Ship Cove. It may also be genetic. After all, she takes after her aunt Annie who, at eighty-four, is still there to make sure Dolores's butter is up to the family standard. The industry standard for butter is 80 percent butterfat content. Dolores keeps hers at about 83 percent, just like her aunt. That's what gives their butter its rich creamy taste and texture. "She loves all this," says Dolores affectionately. "The older people, when they taste it, say my butter is just like my aunt's," she adds with pride.

COURTING SUCCESS

CAROL DENMAN

By Laura Pratt

ANDREW DANSON

Carol Denman is fond of a saying that goes something like this: "If I'd known then what I know now, I would never have taken the risk." The risk in question involved Denman's choice to surface from a devastating blow to the beginning of her independent professional life. In February 1987, her new partner — Ross Atchison — dropped dead and left her holding the bag of liabilities. The pair, whose firm Atchison & Denman Court Reporting Service Ltd. was the one Denman heads today, had no formalized partnership agreement or insurance, and they'd just moved into new premises. The five-year lease — at $5,000 a month — and more than $35,000 in furniture and equipment costs were secured with large personal guarantees. Denman, who lacked security of any kind, was thrown into a panic. One day she left her car running all day, locked, on a downtown Toronto street. She felt scared of the unknown, she says, "like there was some monster lurking beneath the surface I hadn't thought of."

More than a decade later, Denman, forty-seven, has tamed her monsters. Today, she is head of a lucrative court-reporting firm on University Avenue in Toronto. A recipient of a 1993 Canadian Woman Entrepreneur of the Year Award, she employs five permanent office staff and twenty-five freelance court reporters — mostly women — whose business it is to record the evidence presented at examinations for discovery, royal commissions, arbitrations, and hearings. Freelancers are expected to provide their own equipment (typically a Stenotype machine, real-time software, laptop computer and laser printer, and a high-speed modem). They're paid approximately $150 per day for attendance, and anywhere from $3.35 to $6 per page for transcripts, depending on their turnaround time. A really productive reporter can make from $70,000 to $100,000 per year.

In 1997, Denman installed a full video-conferencing centre in her downtown office so now, if a lawyer wants to examine a witness in Hong Kong, she can swear in that person in Toronto — and do the transcript, to boot. Hers is the only court-reporting firm she knows of that offers this service. Next, she's expanding the business, taking over her office's entire floor, and moving into mediation and arbitration work. In 1996, Denman's firm billed some $2 million, a 1,049 percent increase over 1986, the year her company started. She pays herself $60,000 plus a dividend each year-end, depending on "what the accountants" tell her. She keeps most of the profit in the company and doesn't have any bank loans, debt, or lines of credit.

Court reporters are the people you see in courtrooms with masks over their faces and funny, adding-machine-like devices at their tapping fingertips. In Canada, they're either Ministry of the Attorney General employees or freelancers with private firms. Denman was a reporter herself for ten years with the Supreme Court of Ontario. Her first case, a first-degree murder trial, "was really very difficult. I had never taken evidence from a pathologist before and I'd never worked with a jury. But I was just enthralled with the whole process. It was like being on 'Perry Mason.'"

Court reporting is tough work. You have to be able to type as fast as someone can speak — albeit on a shorthand-based typewriter — and stay on top of the interruptions, overlaps of conversation, and technical language that characterize a legal proceeding. When Denman was in Grade 9, her mother insisted that her eldest child take typing, so she would "have a skill." Today, Denman's happy for the advice, "considering I can pretty much type faster than anyone in the world." Court reporting is all about processing the sound and keeping two or three words in your head so you can play catch-up when one of the breathless lawyers arranges a dramatic pause. "It's like playing the piano by ear," Denman says. The really interesting testimony is harder to take than the boring stuff, in her opinion, because you start to think about it and then it slows you down.

But a decade of litigation took its toll. "It was murder and rape, murder and rape, murder and rape every day," she sighs. The other drawback of the job was the constant travel, which diverted Denman's attention from her two little boys, Tony and Michael, now nineteen and seventeen. (She also has two step-daughters, with second husband Tom Dunne.) On the way back from one of her frequent away-from-home assignments in the early 1980s, a sappy song called "I'm Just Sitting Here Watching Bobby Grow" came on the radio, and Denman collapsed into tears. "I said, I can't do this any more."

So Denman applied for a leave of absence to teach herself the cutting edge of court-reporting technology: computer-aided transcription. CAT allows reporters to translate from the Stenotype language into English and then convert the whole transcript onto a computer disc for print-out. This system is a far cry from the days when stenographers took six weeks to transcribe their shorthand-recorded transcripts.

Her leave was refused on a Friday. On Monday, she was scheduled to begin reporting a drug trial in a courthouse across the street from the hospital where seven-year-old Tony was being treated for gastroenteritis. So she quit her $70,000-a-year job. "Everybody thought I was out of my mind. And people thought I left to start my own business, that I had this great master plan. That's not true. I quit to work from home, to be self-employed, to make my own hours."

Over the next six months, between loads in the laundry room, Denman transcribed examinations for discovery for the lawyers she'd connected with in her Supreme Court days. Thanks to the dismantling of legislation that said examinations could be reported only by official examiners, Denman was among the first court reporters to get into that market. And business boomed.

"As I got more and more busy, I realized I was getting too distracted working at home," she says. After all, she had never intended to be an at-home mom without a career. "If I hadn't worked, I would have been one of those mothers who expect their kids to speak three languages by the time they're five. I would have driven them absolutely crazy, because I have so much energy." When Ross Atchison came along in search of a partner in February 1986, Denman decided to go for it. Atchison would be the firm's financial and administrative brain; Denman would focus on the work.

A year later, two weeks after moving into their 25,000-square-foot office, forty-five-year-old Atchison dropped dead of an aneurysm.

Aside from a stint in Moncton when she was ten, selling lemonade to construction workers for two cents a glass, Denman's first job was filing insurance claims for the Civil Service Federation in Ottawa when she was fifteen (she lied about her age). She went to university — University of Toronto — for just a year, and only then because she was awarded a scholarship. "What good are science and geometry going to do me when all I want to do is make a buck?" Denman remembers thinking. She tried her hand at advertising sales, but couldn't get into the shmoozy cocktail parties. When she was twenty, she landed a two-year stint as a conference coordinator with Trudeau's Great Plains Project, a national think-tank. On assignment in Churchill, Manitoba, she met a pair of court reporters and was immediately captivated. "These guys could write as fast as anybody could talk," she says. "And then when we got their bill, I said this is something I'd like to do."

Today, three storeys above the honking, light-glinting city, Carol Denman explains that it's not all about money and material wealth. "It has to do with achievement, self-esteem, success, and having lots of energy," she says, her lake-blue eyes blazing. If she could do it all again, she laughs, she'd start her own bank for all the "little ladies" who run their own businesses. Or at least that's the story she tells backwards executives who invite this novelty businesswoman to tell her quaint tales. A female client once asked Denman, "What is it that you do here? Do you make the photocopies, get the coffee?" Another time, after Denman's speech at a bank meeting admonishing the old boys' network for their unacceptable treatment of female colleagues, the bank manager got up and said, "Thank you very much, Carol, I really enjoyed your speech. And I know something about entrepreneurship because my wife has a little business." The next day, Denman's bank contact called, and she asked him how things were "at the little bank." Clients of her husband, a civil litigation lawyer, frequently inquire of her whether she can make a living with a little court-reporting business. "I say, 'Yeah, two million a year. I can make a living.'"

Denman, who uses her surname from her first marriage for her business and her kids, grew up in a family that moved a lot, to accommodate her dad's position as a general manager for GM in the Maritimes and a car rental agent in Ottawa and Calgary. Denman attended about eighteen different schools. "It was always being the new girl, and I liked that because it was a chance to start over." Carol's brother George calls her Elvis, because she's the family star.

But Elvis crashed when her partner died. Her lowest point was New Year's Day, 1988. She limped into the new year by herself, drilling tables together at the new office space she'd rented, feeling utterly terrified, lonely, overwhelmed. Denman had bought out Atchison's estate and become the sole shareholder. "I guess I was too naïve to know I should pack it in," she says. "I didn't even know I had that option." But she did know she had a stack of liabilities and absolutely no business experience to go with them. "All of a sudden I was running the joint. I had a company and employees and I didn't know the difference between a receivable and a payable."

Denman had phoned all her clients to tell them of her partner's death and to boost their confidence. "From a practical point of view, people aren't going to change their appointments. It's a matter of inconvenience and rescheduling. If they found chaos and if I wasn't coping and the coffee wasn't as good as it used to be, then there would have been a problem."

She asked her reporters, most of whom were older and more business-wise than she, if they'd stick by her and help pull the company through. All six of them said yes. Finally, she set about learning the basics of running a business under the tutelage of some patient accountants. "I still don't know what a lot of things mean," she admits. "But if you're making a profit, you don't have to know, and I was always making a profit."

She was also making a lot of mistakes, but she'd rather not regard them as such. "I think of them as experiences." Her biggest pitfall was getting tied into everyone else's agenda and trying to run a business like a family. When her company installed voicemail and some of her reporters rose up to complain about its impersonality, Denman came to a turning point. "I thought, I am a leader, my name's on the door. Reporters weren't realizing that I have no obligation to give them work." She sat them down and told them she was there to clear up a misperception that she was the mother hen and they were the chicks. "It's not an us-and-them situation," she said. "'Each one of you is competing with each other for work, and the best person will get the best assignments for the best price. I do not have to distribute it fairly.' That was the worst day of my life. I think one of the hard things about it was becoming hard in business without becoming hard personally. My mom used to always say, 'Carol, you're going to become tough,' and I'd say, 'No, I'm not, I'm always going to be the same. But business is tough.'"

Ten years from now, Denman wants "to be making $20,000 a pop doing public speaking." She aims to fill a hole. "I don't know any women in business who go out and talk about women and entrepreneurship. You've got Maureen Kempston Darkes and Shelagh Whittaker, but they're with big businesses. There isn't anybody who's had the experiences I've had. And I had no role model. I don't know any other woman in business who's doing better than I am. So the best thing that I can do is be a role model myself."

STAYING IN STYLE
EVELINE CHARLES

By Liane Faulder

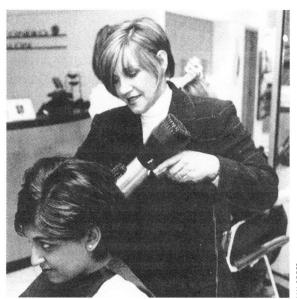

IAN SCOTT

BiancoNero hair salon and spa appears the picture of high fashion to customers walking in the front door. The entrance is framed in a shade of cool, metallic taupe that blends into the marbled tile within. At the front desk, wafer-thin receptionists with French manicures and lips dark as plums check the bookings, while nearby, stylists waft about tired clients, gently sculpting style and expensive streaks from middle-class mops.

But where I sit, in the back of the shop, it's different. It's hot back here — hot, sweaty, and cramped. That's in part because the area is dominated by an enormous steel dryer furiously tumbling towels. As well, the small space, which contains both the staff eating area — a stool near the microwave — and a computer desk, is filled by stylists comparing notes on the new fruit-and-soup diet sweeping the salon.

Something else contributes to the slightly frenetic feel of the back room. It's the owner of BiancoNero, the one responsible for both the high-fashion image and the sweaty reality of this $1.8-million-a-year business. Her name is Eveline Charles, and frankly, I find her a bit scary.

Maybe it's her reputation for playing hard ball in a business famous for flakiness. Maybe it's the way she talks; her speech is fast, gravel-toned, and intense, ideas spurting in a throaty burst of words.

Or maybe it's because she walks so fast and does so much at once that it's just plain hard to keep up with her.

Whatever the reason, I never lose the sensation that there is a powerful force in the room whenever we get together to talk about how she took her business from a two-chair salon in a small northern Alberta town to a major player in Edmonton's growing health and beauty market.

Charles — fashionable in a no-nonsense black suit and chunky boots — is hunched over the computer crammed against the wall, talking advertising numbers with her newly hired sales director. At the same time, she scoops a mouthful of the miracle soup into her mouth while checking the clock behind her. Charles is in a rush — a half-hour ago she was supposed to be in her own spa for a Cleopatra milk bath, something she hasn't found time for since the spa expanded to include luxury water treatments in September 1996.

But she's okay with being late. Charles is in a good mood and she's going with the flow, laughing and talking with staff. Her cheerful banter is rooted, at least in part, in a minor business coup. The night before, she scored $30,000 worth of advertising for only $9,000 in a local fund-raising auction by the advertising community.

"This takes care of the spring advertising budget," she says, grinning ear to ear as she scoots around the back room on a rolling red plastic desk chair. She looks right at me, as if to explain her Cheshire smile. "I need to win every day," she says. "If I can't win every day, I'm not happy."

The longer I'm with Eveline Charles, the more I see she lives those words. She has a framed poem on the desk of her office, a clutter of invoices and plastic bottles with generic labels (BiancoNero is in the process of launching its own product line).

The poem is called "The Winner" and Charles stumbled on it while training for her first marathon in 1995. The verse has a certain Hallmark-card flavour, but it reflects Charles's sentiments. "Think big and your deeds will grow. Think small, and you fall behind."

You need an attitude like that to move from Fahler, Alberta (population 1,200), to run a business that grew in revenue by 300 percent in the 1996 fiscal year. It's an attitude born when Charles was a small girl and learned if you want to get by, never mind get ahead, you have to push. Hard.

Born in 1953 to a French-Canadian/Dutch farming family, Eveline Veraart was the eldest daughter of six kids, and she was "expected to do everything."

Charles had a lot of responsibility at a young age; her parents had little money, and wages from her first job — washing dishes at the age of thirteen — went directly to pay family bills. "I remember worrying as a kid if there was enough money for the phone and groceries," says Charles.

But she was born with a relentless energy. "I could never sit still," she recalls one night as we talk in the kitchen of her $270,000 home in St. Albert, an Edmonton bedroom community. Her husband, Canadian Airlines pilot Barry Charles, works on the computer in his office down the hall. Their boys buzz around the kitchen table; two-year-old Max clatters by on a ride-on toy, in search of the nanny. Taylor, a nine-year-old as bright and busy as his mom, is eager to share an alarming invention, a slingshot crafted from elastics and bits of old toys.

As if in preparation for the juggling act that is small business, Charles had a lot on the go, even as a teenager. She learned to stretch a dollar by sewing clothes and cutting hair for herself and her friends. By the age of eighteen, she was working four jobs. She sold popcorn at the local theatre and worked at the Adanac Hotel (Canada spelled backwards) as a chambermaid, waitress, and bartender.

In a town dominated by blue jeans and small dreams, Eveline stood out. Her hair was dark, but she dyed her bangs blonde, wore platform shoes and mini-skirts. And she was a bit wild — sneaking out the bedroom window only to be brought back home by police was just her sort of teenage prank. At twenty-one, she bought a metallic grey Corvette — scandalous in Fahler. "I always did my own thing and was independent," she says.

She balanced a rebellious nature with a need to succeed. Charles's aunt, Beatrice Vandel, owned the town theatre, a grocery store, and a hardware store. "I looked up to her. I always knew I'd have my own business, too. Someday."

Launching a salon was a natural move for Charles; she had a reputation in town for being creative and fashionable and a talent for knowing what suited customers. At the age of twenty-one, with $1,000 borrowed from her dad, she opened a shop in the Adanac called Place for Hair where she painted everything a bold red, white, and blue. It was the only shop in town with a trendy shag carpet. At twenty-six, though she had built up a business to include clients who came all the way from Peace River (an hour's drive away), she decided it was time to leave Fahler. There had been a marriage at twenty-one to the town's prize catch, the hotel owner's son, and a divorce at twenty-three. Charles wanted to move on. She locked the shop doors in 1980 and, with $3,000 in her pocket, moved to Edmonton.

Well, a suburb of the big city. Although Charles has always had substantial dreams, she's a prudent financial manager who takes things one step at a time. She found a $20,000 shop called Hair Focus in St. Albert and bought it with a $17,000 bank loan co-signed by a friend.

St. Albert was good for Eveline; she learned how to put clients through that chair at a wicked pace — often on her feet from 7 a.m. to 9 p.m. "I never said no to a client who walked through that door."

Four years later, Charles had three full-time stylists and one part-time. The business was debt-free and bringing in $180,000 a year. But frankly, Charles wanted more than the suburbs could offer. "In St. Albert, the women all had small children and big mortgages. Nobody had any money. I wanted to be downtown."

Downtown was Holt Renfrew, glass skyscrapers, and corporate clients willing to spend big bucks (today, her top clients spend between $2,000 and $4,000 a year on hair at BiancoNero). In 1984, Charles sold Hair Focus, pocketing $5,000 in profit, and formed a partnership with one of her stylists, Roy Semkow. The two came up with one-third of the money required for a $110,000 renovation on a small, second-floor shop in a downtown office tower. The bank and the building owner put up the rest. Charles called the shop BiancoNero (Italian for white and black) because it conveyed the trendy European image she was trying to establish.

By 1989, BiancoNero had expanded to six stylists, and Charles was ready for a larger salon in Edmonton Centre, one of two downtown malls. Sure, the rent was steep — three times that in the suburbs. But the high-traffic location attracted enough shoppers to cover the difference; business doubled to $700,000 in the first year. At the same time, the partners expanded to Calgary; Semkow wanted to get out of Edmonton. The partnership dissolved shortly thereafter. "It was just too hard to keep things going, being in two different cities," says Charles.

The idea for a European-style spa came in 1995. It was shortly after Charles moved from the third floor at Edmonton Centre to a better location — two shops across the hall from each other — on the second floor.

It was a big move, costing $500,000. Using the family home as collateral, Charles got a $150,000 bank loan. She had saved $100,000 in cash from the salon, and mall management kicked in $250,000 in leasehold improvements.

Like many entrepreneurs with more ideas than resources, Charles admits she went into the new effort short of cash. The move required $100,000 worth of inventory she didn't quite have the money to buy, so she talked the supplier into spreading payments over three months instead of the usual up-front outlay.

"I just hoped we were busy. And we were," she says. BiancoNero brings in between $150,000 and $180,000 a month, half of which goes to payroll.

No sooner were they settled than Charles began to think bigger. The new location featured a couple of body treatment rooms on one side, but Charles decided if she wanted to corner the health and wellness market in Edmonton, she needed more.

She was training for a marathon at the time, one of four she ran that year. That winter, rising at 5:30 a.m. to train outside regardless of icy streets and brutal Edmonton temperatures, she began to feel her strength building, physically and mentally. "I pushed myself with those marathons, farther than ever. It became like mind over matter. Push. Push. Push. And I knew I could do anything," she recalls.

Then she heard someone else in the city was planning a luxury spa. "That really burned me. I got a lump in my stomach. I thought: Oh shit. I can't lose that niche. I'm really competitive that way." So she turned up the heat and in the spring of 1996 expanded again, which cost an additional $350,000 — $200,000 from the bank, $30,000 from mall management, and the rest in cash from the business.

Today, her luxury day spa glistens with the sparse, almost clinical air common in a European health resort, where wellness is next to godliness. A large glass-topped table in the client relaxation area is graced with an enormous vase of white lilies; the $10,000 Vichy water chamber (complete with a fire hose for those persistent back kinks) where I undergo a rose body scrub sparkles like an operating theatre.

Charles didn't have aesthetics at BiancoNero — which now consumes 7,000 square feet of the mall — before the expansion. She needs a whole new client base to fill those sixteen treatment rooms, but that doesn't worry her. "Our goal is to turn all our hair clients into spa clients. We're also going after the hotel and convention market. And I think we can build half the spa business through gift certificates," says Charles, who sold $130,000 worth of gift vouchers at Christmas. "We've just hired a full-time sales manager to hit the downtown office market — gift certificates are a great staff incentive at the corporate level."

Charles is counting on aggressive marketing — in 1996, Charles sunk $100,000 into advertising, up from $3,000 the previous year — to imprint BiancoNero on the minds of Edmontonians.

"I know how to make money," says Charles with confidence. "I'd sweep the streets to make my business work." Charles is famous in the Edmonton salon community for her combination of hair-cutting talent and sheer, dogged drive. Though she recently cut back to styling only two days a week, she still spins about twenty-five clients through each day, pulling in between $1,500 and $2,000 a day in cuts, colours, and conditioners.

Stylists who have worked for her agree; she's fast, she's good, and she's pushy. Once you're in her chair, she moves into "upsell" — tantalizing clients with expensive streaks, or a perm, where the salon makes big money. She's also not shy to promote products such as wooden hair brushes branded with the BiancoNero logo.

"I don't like to hear the word no," she admits. "If someone says no to me, I just want it more."

The attitude carries over to home life. When her husband was reluctant to have a second child, Charles just kept at him till he broke down. "Barry will tell you himself, I drive him crazy."

"Eveline is a make-work project," admits Barry, laughing. She's always in a hurry, often leaving a visible trail as she whirls through the day. There was the time she couldn't wait for the garage door to be completely open and tore it off backing out of the garage. "That took me a day and a half to fix," says Barry.

And Eveline is absent-minded. Barry recalls the winter day she wasn't paying attention while snow-blowing the driveway and blew all the snow directly into the garage. But he admires her drive and her fearless nature. "We're both survivors," says Barry, who also came from a home where money was scarce.

The two don't see a lot of each other; Barry is often in the sky, and in the last two years, Eveline has nearly lived at the shop. But candlelit dinners aren't a priority for this couple. Barry says they enjoy each other the most when they're taking on a challenge together, such as hiking or windsurfing. Eveline is still the caregiver in her large, close-knit extended family, and Sundays are often devoted to roast beef suppers at the Charles home. As well, Barry and Eveline can afford to take big holidays with the boys; Eveline pays herself a gross salary of $164,000 year.

Barry, a slim, athletic red-head, recalls the first time he saw his wife-to-be, more than ten years ago. Barry, a clean-cut, conservative air force pilot, was in the parking lot of an Edmonton lounge when Eveline wheeled around the corner in her trademark grey Corvette.

"That car had been around the block a few times," he remembers. "It was scratched and the muffler was dragging. But there was Eveline, her head cranked out the window, a cigarette hanging out of her mouth." He leans back in his chair, arms over his head, chuckling at the recollection. "She had almost no hair. I guess it was in style to shave your head."

The two began to date, and then it looked like Barry might be transferred to a base elsewhere in Canada. "I told him, I'm not going with you," recalls Eveline. "I wasn't going to be some army guy's wife, stuck on a God-forsaken base up north." Barry quit the air force and they got married.

Barry has been instrumental in helping the business grow in the past few years. A jack of all trades, Barry volunteers to do everything from installing BiancoNero's new $50,000 computer system to writing the payroll package. He plunges toilets and changes light bulbs. "I can't stand to see the shop paying lots of money for something that would take me five minutes to do," he says. But he admits he's sick of having his time consumed by the business. And as for family life — "That's been a tough thing," he says. Eveline says she's hardly seen their youngest; his birth coincided with the shop's big expansion.

Barry and Eveline know the only way she'll be able to wring more personal time from her life is to quit doing everything herself. But Charles has a hard time convincing other people to work as hard as she does, and she knows high productivity has always been a big part of BiancoNero's success.

"People are lazy today," she says. "They don't want to work hard. Lots of people are happy just to work a little." Charles doesn't put up with what she perceives as laziness and she's not afraid to make people do it her way. She reviews her stylists' numbers every day — how many clients they're bringing in, how much product they sell, and how often they persuade customers to invest in perms, streaks, and so forth. If their numbers are too low, she lets them know.

"Eveline expects 110 per cent and if you're not willing, she doesn't want you. She tells you that. It's sink or swim here — usually within ninety days," says stylist Ashley Harrison. But staff — even the disaffected who have left — say Charles taught them how to make money. Harrison is just one of several among BiancoNero's twenty-one stylists making more than $60,000 a year.

It's not that Charles pays her staff more than other salons. In fact, the 40 to 50 percent commission she offers is less than the 50 to 60 percent of a suburban shop. "Stylists come to me and say, 'I could get 70 percent at this other salon,'" says Charles. "I tell them, 'Go ahead. Seventy percent of nothing is still nothing.'"

Charles keeps her stylists with a high volume of clients generated by the BiancoNero image, which is plastered on billboards all over town and seen on television, too. (Charles produces all her own advertising to save money.) Between 100 and 200 clients a day come through the shop, which is open from 7:30 a.m. to 9 p.m. six days a week.

Former staff complain it's a "cut 'em up, get 'em out" approach to styling that demands a killer pace and leaves clients miffed. But Harrison says that's not true; Charles has taught him expert time management. "It simply doesn't take an hour to cut a client's hair. If you're good, you can do it in half that time," he says, adding BiancoNero has several stylists who have left for other shops, only to return to the fold.

Ask Charles for her business tips and she's quick to point out owners should never let staff think they are too important to you. "When people know you need them, then you're held hostage. It's better for them to be in need of you, rather than the other way around." Charles smiles to hear herself described as tough. "You don't get to fifty staff on the payroll without being tough," she says.

Through her cost-cutting skills, strong vision, and fearless nature, Eveline hopes to push profits to 20 percent in 1997. She knows such ambition — she's also in the process of opening a discount salon in Edmonton Centre — will still require sixty- to seventy-hour weeks. "But I have a lot of energy. People say, 'Is she a machine?' But I'm not a normal person. I don't get tired."

That is, she didn't *used* to get tired. But her husband says Eveline doesn't sleep well these days; too much on her mind. And although Eveline usually never gets sick, she's had four bad colds this year. Barry plans to take a two-month leave of absence this summer so he can regroup and spend time with the children. Eveline plans to join him, but holidays have been cancelled before because of the business.

The larger and more complex the business becomes, the more firm its grip on the owner. "If anything, Eveline is even more committed than I've ever seen her before," says Barry.

He smiles ruefully when he talks about trying to squeeze more family time into their lives: "There are no guarantees."

DESIGNING FOR SUCCESS
LINDA LUNDSTRÖM

By Laura Pratt

Everywhere, there are flashes of gold, dangling strips of leather, and a parade of frosted coifs. Everyone is long and lean. Over Inuit singer Susan Aglukark's taped strains, the crowd — all buyers from haute-couture women's wear shops — talks price points and hemlines. Then the lights dim in this huge back room of the design studio, and the Laparka 1997 Showtime Program begins.

"Linda Lundström Ltd. is a company that chooses to be unique," the host emphasizes. And, with that, a burst of beauties in pale pink — Lundström's own pearl plush — appears. This designer's secret is in the layers — the Nanook look, shed like onion peelings. Flowing, swirling, flatteringly loose, the line of clothes that unfolds before our eyes this winter day is classic Lundström. The skiwear is "multiconvertible and multifunctional." The Jack Frost jerseys, trapeze tops, and retro pants are glamorously casual. In approval, pages flip, flashbulbs burn, and heads bob. By the end of the show, the bevy of buyers who had jockeyed for the best parking spots at this northeast Toronto house of fashion have circled and starred their programs to distraction. "Now it's time," says Linda Lundström, when she appears on stage, "for the real work to begin." A husky, ice-blonde, five-foot, ten-inch-tall daughter of Scandinavian parents ("I look Scandinavian, which certainly hasn't hurt me over the years: in this business it's always helpful when you can stand out"),

Lundström plays the crowd with style. Her two little girls, both decked out in their mother's designs, clamour to claim her. Her husband, Joel Halbert, who's the company's chief financial officer, leads me back to her office, a cluttered space whose proud centrepiece is a "standing desk," because chairs, it turns out, are obstacles to the natural flow of Linda Lundström's creativity.

Officially, the flow began in a two-bedroom brownstone Toronto apartment more than two decades ago, in September 1974, when Lundström decided it was as good a time as any to hit the runways with what she'd learned from two years at Sheridan College's fashion school in Ontario, a couple of stints with Toronto dressmakers, and a year on a prestigious scholarship studying her trade in Europe. Overseas, she says, she learned how to grade patterns, to have a reverence for good food, and how to design, in that order. One bedroom stored the rolling racks. The other was the sewing room. Lundström dyed her own laces in the kitchen. She filled the hallway with boxes bound for shipment. In the dining room, below the wooden plate ledge, she squeezed in a cutting table. And, in the "showroom," there was a Hide-A-Bed where Lundström slept at night. "I'm not a tidy person, so it was a real challenge to keep that room neat." Her first line was "a wardrobe," rather than any particular specialty. Numbering a dozen or so pieces, it included a whole family of products, "everything from head to toe." The initial pieces were sole projects, but Lundström hired two employees within her first month. Sales that first year totalled $14,700, from an initial $10,000 which she says with a snap of her fingers, "went like that. I didn't know there was such a thing as a line of credit at a bank so, for two years, I ran an overdraft, which I was paying huge interest on." The $10,000 was a loan from Lundström's parents with "no strings attached. They really believed in me. I was twenty-three."

One of the biggest mistakes young entrepreneurs make, she believes, is asking the wrong people for help and allowing that misplaced trust to sabotage the business. Another is expecting too much, too fast. "I made a lot of sacrifices in the beginning. I didn't draw a salary for three years. It was very, very slow. When something didn't work, I wouldn't try it again. If it did work, I would. But the underlying theme was my patience. It wasn't a matter so much of 'if' as a matter of 'when.'"

Lundström modelled her new company on the best principles of the companies she'd worked for, chief among them — common sense. She's never read books about management techniques, she boasts, and she's never attended seminars on how to run companies. The kick for Linda Lundström comes from figuring things out for herself. In the beginning, it was "extremely challenging." She worked very hard — seven days a week — and forsook a social life. She went for a year and a half without a single date. "I was working, working, working — and I loved every minute of it. Well, I didn't love every minute of it. But, looking back on it now, I just had to do it. I was totally consumed with this need to get this company going. The greatest challenge was keeping some kind of balance in my life. And money — cash flow was always a problem for me."

She sought customers through pavement pounds in which she assessed the retail landscape to identify the stores she wanted to sell to, and then calling them up with an invitation to come by and view her wares. Only one person came. "It was very slow," she sighs. "Baby steps." After that, she starting trudging around the stores herself, garments slung over her arm.

She survived the recession by emphasizing quality over quantity. Indeed, she believes the pressure made her stronger. "When the wolf was at the door, I felt more creative and took more risks. And I basically ignored the wolf." The scariest time was in the late 1970s, when the Bank of Nova Scotia came within hours of calling her loan because she didn't have the capital to finance her growth. The skin of her teeth and some clever footwork pulled her through. "The banks never believed in me, but I did."

Lundström's breakthrough really came in the mid-eighties, when she developed the Laparka line. More recently, sales have increased as a result of a successful foray into the United States. Competition bothers this designer not at all. In fact, she claims to have no idea who her competition is. Her positioning: "To be unique in everything we do." Her biggest influences are real women with real lives and real bodies. Lundström, who is part of all her company's initial designs at "sunrise meetings," recently cancelled her subscriptions to fashion magazines so she could stop worrying about what she was supposed to be designing and concentrate on what felt right. She describes her own clothing style as "soft, flowing, easy-fitting, body-skimming, comfortable, colourful and feminine." She wears only her clothes, from inside out, and especially enjoys making clothes that flatter a particular body type — she introduced "plus" sizes in 1996 — or fill a special need such as mastectomy swimwear. Lundström is also inspired by colour, an aspect of design she feels is underrated for its effect on how it makes one feel. In the shop, she's started covering all her temperamental sewing machines in turquoise silk. Now they don't break down nearly as much. "I don't know if the turquoise silk is making them work better, but it's pretty to look at." Fabric choices are based on their "personality, depth, fluidity, and drape." Lundström won't buy until she's held something up to a mirror to see how it falls.

Today, Lundström, who can wear turquoise and also butterscotch but looks terrible in black, will clear $15 million in sales, a 25 percent increase over last year's $12 million. Success has also arrived by way of industry recognition: Lundström's list of awards is long, topped off with the 1996 Entrepreneur of the Year Award from the North York Chamber of Commerce, the 1995 Order of Canada, and the 1994 Lifetime Achievement Award from the Canadian Woman Entrepreneur of the Year Awards and the University of Toronto. "But twenty-three years is a long time to get to the sales volume I have," she admits. Her fingers crawling across her standing desk, she says, "I'm the tortoise, not the hare. It's not that I'm slow, but I'm really steady." Indeed, she needs to consult the calculator to even hazard a guess at what a 25 percent hike over last year's number will produce. Figures, financially speaking, are not her strong suit. "We all come into this world with a lot of things in our toolbox, and I've got some really high-precision tools in mine.

But there are still lots of things I'm missing." (In the beginning, she had accountants coming out of her ears managing her books for her.) Everybody, Lundström says, poking at her gut, has a toolbox of attitudes, beliefs, and skills they carry with them throughout their lives.

It's in search of complementary tools to her own that this design carpenter hires her staff. "I love working around people who can really focus and work hard," she explains. "I love working around people who are resourceful. I love working around people who are willing to put in some effort, who have enthusiasm and energy. But, most of all, I love working around people who are different than I am. There's not enough time, and there's too much to do. So my biggest challenge is to be constantly mentoring and developing people around me that can support my unique ability, so that I can zero in on the things I love to do."

Once found, these employees are placed in Lundström's personnel-friendly hands. Lundström staff is paid, in part, from a profit-sharing plan. Last year, the firm distributed over 20 percent of profits to the employees. But a person's salary, the president says, is only one component of what he or she values in a job. It's all the qualitative things, Lundström believes, the things that are never measured on a financial statement or payroll sheet, that make her employees rich. The company's "wellness policy" allows employees to take care of personal things, such as dentists' appointments and sick kids home from school. "Balance in life is really important to us," she says. She doesn't encourage people to work overtime. No company functions take place on non-company time. And attendance at any company-related activities that crop up during off hours is completely voluntary. A 1994 paper on Lundström's company by a graduate student at York University's Faculty of Administrative Studies drew a distinction between the "work-holism" she witnessed there — where work is an extension of self — and "workaholism" — where work is impinging on self. "I don't see myself as a designer of clothes," Lundström says. "I see myself as a designer of a company."

Twenty-three years after it began, Lundström's design project is at least 110 people strong (the numbers shoot up during summer production seasons). Among them are four full-time salespeople, with a back-up team of nine, twenty-two in-factory sewers, and approximately thirty-five home workers. It's based in a 37,000-square-foot sprawl of a space, the company's fourth location and soon to be left behind in favour of a fifth. Linda Lundström Inc. produces 122,000 garments a year, made up of four lines (Laparka is shown to buyers in January and hits the stores in the summer; the fall line comes out in February and stores get it in August or September; Goddess gear — hot-weather wear for snowbirds — is shown in May and arrives at the retail level in November or December; and the spring collection shows in August or September and reaches stores in the first three months of the year). Lundström policy insists on a minimum order from every retailer interested in selling her styles. That, she says, is because so much effort is put into developing a collection of clothes that co-ordinate. "A retailer has to represent the line properly. If you break up the family, it doesn't make sense." Most Lundström retailers, she boasts, have a following of loyal clients who are always coming in to see what's new. "And because we're retailers ourselves, we've found out more about the challenges facing retailers — and constantly getting new merchandise is key."

Linda Lundström operates four retail stores in the Toronto area. Besides that, there are shops in Kitchener, Edmonton, Vail, and Aspen that sell only Linda Lundström merchandise, but which the designer doesn't have any part of. All told, some 500 stores across North America carry some representations of Lundström. The company has also shipped to Europe ("I ran into a woman walking down the street the other day wearing a Laparka," laughs Lundström, "and she told me she bought it in Amsterdam"), but because its American business is growing well, Lundström has chosen to concentrate on the American rather than the European market.

Throughout the company, there is a very deliberately woven common thread: a recognition of native heritage. Until she was seventeen, Lundström lived with her parents and two older sisters in Cochenour, a little town in a northern Ontario gold-mining district called Red Lake, where her father worked as a miner with his own company, R. Lundström Contracting. As if to prove it, Lundström insists I follow her out to the office's front area, where a vast piece of stretched hide stamped with a Canadian map greets visitors. There, she points out her home town, the one location highlighted on the map — with a pin and a feather. When Lundström lived there, about 70 percent of the Red Lake district was native. "Not only did I witness racism, but I actually participated in it, I'm ashamed to say. What we studied in school was our culture, not theirs. It was like they were invisible." She didn't come to terms with this shame until she was in her thirties. "I had a cathartic experience," she says, with a fist-slam to the desk and a practised tone to her voice that suggests a retelling. "It made me realize I was carrying a lot of guilt. It was almost like my conscience was aching." The epiphany occurred some ten years ago while she was watching Peter Gzowski interview on television the founder of the Canadian Native Arts Foundation, John Kim Bell. They were talking about the wealth of artistic talent that exists in native communities, with no means of support or encouragement. When she heard that, Lundström recalls, sticking a thumb at her chest, "something happened. I realized that, for my own healing, I had to do something positive to try to make amends.

"I thought, here's a people, a nation, that I lived among, and I didn't know anything about them. I didn't even know how to say hello to them in their language. I went up there and said, I want to do whatever it takes to start exposing native and non-native children in the community to the fact that there are two cultures co-existing, which need to be respected equally." Getting a curriculum change would have been too bureaucratic, she says, "so I gave them money." In 1991, Lundström established the Kiishik Fund in Red Lake. All her public-speaking honorariums (she's paid $2,000 per speech) go to the fund, which has as its mission to bring native people into Red Lake classrooms to share their language, art, and traditional ways. Lundström also collaborates on her designs with native artists — women and men from a variety of Canadian native communities — and appliqués their work onto her Laparkas, which makes up some 64 percent of the business. These artists are paid a design fee and a percentage of sales of their products.

Linda Lundström would like to teach her children — two daughters, aged seven and eleven — and her employees to be honest with themselves and with others, and that all people are equal. "And I'd like to give them the gift my mother gave me: the encouragement to find something you love to do, and to do that."

In Cochenour, a kid could swim or skate all day long and fish the evening away on the lake. There were blueberries and mushrooms to be picked, forts to be built, deer to be skinned. The summer she was four, Linda learned to drive the family boat. When she was eleven, her parents trusted her enough to let her and a girlfriend take off across the lake and go camping on their own.

School, admits Lundström, played a distant second to outdoor pursuits. "Sometimes I'd have an exam the next day, and that didn't seem to matter to my mom and dad. They wanted me to do well in school, but it was more important to go out and fish. I don't ever remember being told to do my homework and I don't ever remember them having any expectations of marks. Consequently, I didn't do that well in school, but I did okay in life."

More than anything else about her childhood, Lundström remembers a feeling of freedom. When she was about seven, her mother opened a fabric store in the basement. Armed with two suitcases full of fabric she'd ordered through the Eaton's catalogue, Linda's mother sold them for the price she'd paid. When interested neighbours complained they didn't have sewing machines to put the fabric to use, Lundström's mother bought a slew of Singer sewing machines and rented them out. When the machines came back, Linda would take them apart, clean the parts, and oil them. After school, she'd bolt home to her part-time job in the basement where, she marvels, she had access to patterns, buttons, zippers, and any amount of sewing paraphernalia.

Every couple of years, Red Lake district sponsored a sewing contest. When she was just eight, Lundström entered a pantsuit she'd sewn: a jacket and pants made of cotton chino with a navy and blue houndstooth check against a white background. She won the contest, along with $15 and a mention in the local newspaper. By the time she was fourteen, Lundström was making clothes for other people. "I always felt self-conscious about asking for money. Even today, the whole money end of the business is something I don't really want to have anything to do with. My mom loved doing what she was doing and money wasn't what motivated her. My dad loved being a miner and money was never what motivated him, either. Maybe it's because deep down inside I didn't feel right charging for something that was so much fun."

Lundström credits her Icelandic mother, Olavia — now eighty-one and vice-president of the company — and Swedish father, Richard, with teaching her plenty: to scale fish, to fix machines, to clean spark plugs, to paddle a canoe, to pluck a duck, and to appreciate the value of hard work. Her father used to say, "Hard work will never kill you," and, in daughter Linda's case, it definitely hasn't. "I'm not afraid to try things and I experiment a lot," she says, before adding, "and I make a lot of mistakes."

To be any more specific, she says, would be impossible. "The mistakes are too numerous to mention. In fact, I'm probably going to make one doozy of a mistake today. But it's part of life. If you don't make any mistakes, you don't have the opportunity to learn from those mistakes."

Currently on the blackboard? A lesson about the importance of taking time for self. Married for twelve years, Lundström admits she struggles with an urge to spread herself too thin. She works five days a week, from forty-six to fifty hours. Her husband has recently taught her how to take holidays, but her impulse is always to keep on working. "I would love to stand here and say I've got it all figured out, but I don't," she says. Pacing, she explains that she's found it quite impossible to give what she needs to give at the office, give what she needs to give at home, and be left with anything to give herself. "I start to get really resentful after a while. That I don't have time to paint my nails, even though I didn't like to paint my nails. Just to sit in a hot bath and not have anybody need me for a while. Yes, there's a certain satisfaction in being needed. It's hard to give that up. It's also hard to feel deserving of the things that you need. But this business of feeling that I'm on a muddy highway with no windshield wiper fluid is what I don't want my life to feel like."

For two years now, Lundström's tried to fill her tank with a regular fitness routine. She goes walking for forty-five minutes every morning in the ravines around her house and returns for a swim in a swimmer's treadmill she had installed indoors (a miniature swimming pool with a built-in current to swim against). "Being out in nature is so important to me. And I get some of the best ideas and clarity of thought when I have my head in that pool. I'm the kind of person who gets a lot of stimulation from what's around me: in order to cut it off, I have to get under water." Lundström takes regular vacations, to places like Mexico and the Bahamas, and she visits her cottage in the Caledon Hills every weekend. Next year, she'll take seven weeks off.

Ours is a standing interview and, when we tour the site, passing the heaps of coloured garments and vast machinery, I discover we're not alone in our uprightedness. Lundström proudly points out the "standing desks" she's recently ordered for staff (including one employee who guiltily springs from her chair when her boss delivers a sideways glance). In addition, the phone system has been revamped to make telecommunications hands-free. This way, beams an energized Lundström, headset-adorned employees can perform dual functions, talking on the phone and inspecting the garment-strewn landscape at the same time.

Still, Lundström insists she doesn't impose her own work habits on those who work for her. Her professional proclivities are born from a childhood rife with challenges that demanded adapting strategies be developed. Alongside the freshwater fish and liberation, Lundström grew up with alcohol. Her father, who died a year ago, was a long-standing alcoholic, and her mother became a sympathetic alcoholic for a time, too. Her eyes turn steely as she explains that an alcoholic's children have to grow up fast. They rush in to parent their parents and consequently miss the blissful period when responsibilities are virtually non-existent. Life is unpredictable, and disorder is the norm. As such, Lundström learned to perform best in chaos and to respond promptly to sudden bends in the road. Her mantra, "Flexibility, rock and roll," is spelled out in big letters and pinned on the bulletin board that makes up one of her office walls. She calls the state of anarchy "an exhilarating place to be."

But don't get her wrong: Linda Lundström harbours no regrets about this, or any other part of her life. "Growing up in that kind of household has made me the person I am today," she says. "I developed an ability to be really resourceful. I learned to see the positive in everything, to transform situations into something that works. And all of this has stood me in good stead in business.

"To say I have no regrets sounds really arrogant, like I did everything right. It's not that, it's that when I look back on things, I realize they had to happen in order to become a part of my toolbox. Sometimes the greatest lessons are the ones that you experience through your own tears. Because life is not about not feeling things."

13   **KEEPING A SAFE** HOUSE
EVA HOUSE

By Diana Luckow

In the summer of 1994 when Eva House, president of Tricom Services Inc., sallied out of her office to meet with clients, they were invariably shocked to see her. "I was as bald as a cueball," says House frankly, "and I didn't wear a hat or a scarf or anything else."

Her shorn head wasn't the result of chemotherapy treatments for cancer, as many may have thought. In fact, she'd had her shoulder-length red hair shaved off on a bet to raise money for the cleft palate unit of Vancouver's Children's Hospital. The fund-raiser, which also saw her comptroller and general manager shave their heads, raised $7,000, but it also demonstrated something else. "People found out — don't challenge me," she says with a grin, "because I don't back down very easily."

It's a good thing that House, forty-four, is up to challenges, because she's encountered many in her seven years in business, including the unexpected unionization of some of her employees, a business-throttling computer crash, and now, growing competition in a market in which her company has become a leader. Moreover, she's a woman operating in what has traditionally been a man's world, where the competition can be nasty.

Her primary business, Tricom Emergency Services, based in Burnaby, British Columbia, has grown to become one of the largest alarm-monitoring companies in western Canada. Tricom's alarm station monitors more than 30,000 alarms in British Columbia, Alberta, Ontario, and Washington State for a client base of just under 200 licensed alarm-installing companies. Round-the-clock operators respond to as many as 6,500 alarms in every twenty-four-hour period, contacting the appropriate authorities such as fire stations, ambulances, police, business owners, even parents.

The service doesn't monitor for only break-ins, fire, or emergency medical situations — it also monitors such commercial concerns as ammonia gas levels in chicken barns or overflow levels in sewage treatment plants. Personal monitoring is also becoming popular. Tricom now monitors latchkey kids, contacting parents if a child hasn't come home at the scheduled time and tripped the alarm. "We can monitor anything that you can put a detector on," says general manager Doug House. The company even monitors a rare houseplant for a residential customer who travels frequently. When the moisture level in the pot drops to a predetermined level, the alarm trips and Tricom calls a neighbour to water the plant.

Tricom grew quickly because Eva cleverly identified an untapped market. Her firm provides non-competitive alarm monitoring for independent alarm installers. Before Tricom's entry into the industry, independent installers had to contract out the monitoring service for their alarms to bigger firms that also competed with them for installations. "We're not threatening our clients," says House. "They install and charge a fee for the monitoring service, and we provide the service for them."

It's not the case that in the beginning House sat back, coolly surveyed the security industry, and zeroed in on a great market niche. She was a high-school drop-out who had never excelled in school, who never finished Grade 10, and whose business experience leaned more towards waitressing and switchboard operating, and her venture into the business world was born more out of desperation than design. It all began in the mid-eighties when her husband, Doug House, a paramedic, began running a private, twenty-four-hour, non-emergency, patient-transfer ambulance service. He asked her to help him out in the business, which was cruising on shaky ground. She pitched in, doing radio dispatch and body re-movals, even learning some of the administrative and accounting functions. Still, it wasn't enough. The business, Phoenix Ambulance, continued to founder and Doug took on some business partners.

As is often the case in struggling small businesses, both the marriage and the partnership soured and by September 1989, Doug was locked out of the business — and the marriage. Eva remained working for the partners, who had recently agreed to monitor alarms for an alarm installer who had placed his monitoring equipment on their premises.

Although Eva continued to work for the partners, she says it wasn't a happy arrangement. She was going through the trauma of marital separation and also harboured a lot of anger towards the partners themselves, not only for locking her husband out of the business but also for their business methods, with which she disagreed. When she discovered that the partners weren't much interested in the alarm-monitoring arrangement and were planning to disconnect some of the equipment without informing the installer, she saw an opportunity. She approached the installer, explained the situation, and offered to take over the monitoring herself on different premises. The installer agreed.

Still, House had a problem. She knew the partners would balk if she informed them she was quitting to take over the alarm monitoring. So she found a ten-by-ten-foot office space, asked her estranged husband, Doug, to do some wiring for her and build a plywood counter, and had a friend install a rental phone. Next, she arranged to remove the installer's equipment while the rest of the firm was at the company Christmas party. It was, she admits, a sneaky move but she says, "I've never done anything to the norm in this life, and never will."

With only a $700 final paycheque in her pocket and no savings, Eva found herself monitoring the alarm system twenty-four hours a day, living and sleeping in the ten-by-ten room, and occasionally hiring a part-timer for relief so that she could return to her rented basement suite where she slept on a mattress on the floor. Despite what appeared to be a ridiculous situation, Eva, then thirty-seven, was determined to support herself. "I was in the midst of a separation, and my attitude was that because there'd been hardships in the past, I didn't want to rely on a man to support me. I wanted to do something for myself."

There's irony here, though, because today she runs her company — which she owns entirely — with the able and enthusiastic assistance of Doug, from whom she's been legally separated for the past six years, and of her common-law spouse, Ross Harding, who is the company comptroller and who formerly worked for Phoenix. The three of them have laboured as a team to build Tricom, which now includes a security guard division known as Tricom Security Services and a temporary first-aid attendant service, Medic One First Aid. Together, these companies employ about seventy-five full- and part-time staff working off-premises and represent 50 percent of total business revenues, which hit $3.6 million in fiscal '96.

"It's a partnership of the mind and of the heart, not on paper," says Doug, who acknowledges that their personal and business situation is unique, to say the least. He says it works out fine because "we got to a point in our lives where priorities changed. There wasn't really time for the marriage but the friendship was so valuable that we decided if we carried on the marriage, we would lose the friendship.

"Eva wanted to have more life in the business," he explains. "All of a sudden she discovered the business world and loved it and wanted to go deeper in and found that having a husband got in the way." So, says Doug philosophically, "I changed residences and kept the same employer. She's my best friend." Says Eva simply, "Doug is my employee and my confidant, really. We're good friends."

Eva admits that her obsession with her business has usurped her entire life. She wakes each morning at 4 a.m. to plan her day and arrives at work by 6 a.m., not leaving in the evening until 7 or 8 p.m. and rarely retiring before midnight. "I don't like sleeping," she confesses. "I only do it for necessity."

House has always put her money back into the business and takes very little pay (less than $50,000 per year). It's the same with Doug, who says he'd earn three times more doing the same job anywhere else. So why does he do it? "I'll be taken care of down the road," he says confidently. "And to be very blunt and almost mushy, I love it [the business] and I love her. I'm happy here and that's more important than huge quantities of money."

Doug says Eva's drive to succeed in business has nothing to do with compensating for her lack of education. "It wasn't a matter of proving it to herself," he says. "It was a matter of proving it to someone who wasn't even alive — her father."

Born Eva Holzfuss in Berlin, Germany, Eva came to Canada with her parents at age four and grew up in a very strict household, living in a variety of Quebec mining towns, where her father worked as an electrical foreman in power generation plants. Doug says Eva's father resented having three daughters and no sons and that she grew up in a strict, loveless home where she was constantly told she would never amount to anything.

At school, she had difficulties, to which she attributes her poor English skills. At age seventeen, she was still in Grade 10 and ready for vocational testing in the army when her father died suddenly of a heart attack. At that point, she quit school and found work as a nanny. "I was just that stubborn," she says. "I figured I didn't have him telling me what to do any more."

Today, her business is her life — even her reading is confined to business books. She's not interested in hobbies or sports, nor is she interested in homemaking. "Hell, I hate it in the kitchen," she laughs. "I told my boyfriend, Ross, that if you're with me, don't expect me to be a typical housewife because I'm not — I'd rather sit in the office and be doing work than at home."

Although she would love to have had children, a long-ago abusive boyfriend left her unable to bear children. "When people ask me if I have kids, I usually turn around and tell them, 'No, I've been spayed' — they never know how to answer to that one," says House.

She loves animals and turns to her pets for relaxation. "They don't talk back," she says. Needless to say, though, they're not the usual sort of pet, and they're purposely chosen for their low maintenance. She has always been fascinated by snakes — she finds them soothing — and has a four-year-old Royal python called Zeus. "Snakes are very silky and their movement is fascinating compared to any normal animal," she says. Her Surrey home menagerie also includes a new parrot, a finch, and tanks of both saltwater and freshwater fish.

House's personality and style are best described as "down-to-earth." She has several requisite business suits for necessary occasions but prefers comfort to high fashion; it's not unusual to find her at the office in cowboy boots, leggings, and a long overblouse. Her acrylic nails are her trademark — she airbrushes them with designs, applies gold flakes, emblazons them with the company logo for trade shows. "She's a wild and wacky woman," says business consultant Denise Wallace, who has worked on special projects with House since 1994. "And I mean that in the kindest sense. She's a very good-hearted woman."

In the past, many of her twenty-four station attendants referred to her as the "den mother" and she liked that. "There's one word I do not like people using on me and that's 'boss'," she says. "I don't feel like I'm superior, even though I may have a lot more invested here," she laughs. She'll turn her hand to any job that needs doing around the office, no matter how menial — employees have found her shovelling snow, making coffee, answering phones. When the company was preparing its new premises in 1995, she actually did some of the low-voltage telephone and computer wiring. She sees nothing wrong with turning a hand to what needs doing. "I wouldn't refer to it as a failing," she says. "I just don't want to be looked at as a snot."

So it was all the more galling for her when the twenty-four employees who run her alarm station applied for union certification. She received the news over her fax machine on November 28, 1995, just six months after an incredibly difficult move from 2,300-

square-foot premises to new 7,000-square-foot premises — just a month and a half after her company experienced a crippling, expensive computer crash that randomly destroyed information in thousands of accounts.

"I had no idea the certification was coming," she says. "I was so busy managing from one event to another." She didn't have the vaguest idea of what to do next. "I was scared stiff for the business. I wasn't sure how to talk to the employees. It was like a total wall went up."

More than anything, she was personally hurt by the employees' move to certification. She'd always believed she had a good relationship with her staff. "I had the biggest, broadest shoulders for everybody," she says. That, however, she now believes, led to her undoing.

House had become so caught up in the intricacies of moving a twenty-four-hour operation involving more than 200 phone lines from the old premises to the new that she had less time to involve herself with her staff. She feels they resented that, despite the fact that she had asked for their input and as a result incorporated fifty-nine of the sixty requests they made, including a sauna and gym facility.

"They had input to the colour scheme, even the silk plants," she says as she tours the bright, peach-toned monitoring station, with its many windows, sound-proof rooms for noisy equipment, and ergonomically designed operator "pods."

It took almost a year to sign a collective agreement, and the whole process nearly came to a lock-out. "Out of the whole thing, the employees never gained anything," says House bitterly. "I lost numerous clients and $100,000 to negotiators and lawyers. The employees would have had more in raises under our normal standards — which was at least in the vicinity of 10 percent; now they're at 2 percent. We're now paying their medical but they're paying union dues. And taxes just went up again. So what did they gain?"

House feels that unionization has greatly affected how she runs her company; her former open-door policy is now closed and much of the personal aspect has been taken away. "It's like a death in the family, or losing your kids," she says sadly. And she worries that the policy of union seniority will destroy employee incentive and her ability to advance those who show promise. While she says she has learned a lot from the experience, she wouldn't wish it on her worst enemy.

Although Eva may not have "enemies" in her industry, she has experienced adversity in this fiercely competitive, male-dominated business. For example, when her company changed premises, not all the phone lines were reconnected as they were supposed to be. "So rumour had it that we didn't pay our phone bill," she says. "I had to get a letter from the telephone company to prove to my clients that this was just idle rumour."

When Tricom agreed to act as the test site for a new state-of-the-art line monitoring system for B.C. Telephone, rumour went out that she must be sleeping with someone at the telephone company in return for the opportunity. In fact, it cost Tricom $100,000 to implement the new technology in hopes that it would become the industry standard. It did — with the result that Tricom was using it a year ahead of anybody else.

"I'm finding I'm always having to back myself up, to prove myself," says Eva. "Competition is healthy, but when it's being maliciously done it makes it so that you're constantly having to backtrack on things instead of going ahead." With so much adversity, she's coined a phrase. "We joke about it," she says. "We have an internal word we use — AFLE — Another Frigging Learning Experience — because we've seen so many."

In common with many small businesses, House had difficulty finding the capital to expand her business. "Banks don't believe in you very much when you start the way I did," she says. In the beginning, she had only the $1,000 monthly revenue from her first alarm-monitoring contract. She was wise enough, however, to meet her bank manager at the very beginning to establish a relationship and reputation. When she needed money to fund new equipment, she went back for a chat. "I had no idea what a business plan was," she admits. "I had quite a lot of difficulty even getting something like an overdraft." As a result, all of her initial growth was self-financed through Tricom's cash flow.

By 1991, House needed more space and arranged with the landlord to take over an additional 2,300 square feet of available warehouse. She also decided to become listed by the Underwriters Laboratory of Canada so that she could offer a more sophisticated alarm service acceptable to the big insurance companies. "We wanted to live up to the standard," she explains. For that, however, she needed $60,000 in order to comply with the ULC specifications and equipment.

So she and Doug, who by now had given up on repairing their marriage, sold the house they'd built on Bowen Island and used the $20,000 profit towards meeting the certification requirements. It still wasn't enough, however, so Eva went back to the bank and, after putting up everything she had invested in the business as collateral, they gave her a $40,000 loan. The whole process took two to three months, with about a dozen meetings back and forth. "They weren't handing it out, that's for sure," she says.

By 1994, space was tight again — the volumes were up in the alarm-monitoring station and House had started up the security guard division, Tricom Security Services. She turned to the Business Development Bank of Canada for assistance in obtaining a loan so that she could move into bigger premises. The previous year, she had taken a ten-month course through the BDB called the Step-Up Program for Women in Business and learned about the bank's services and the various financing routes available.

The BDB paired her with management services representative Vaughn Dennis. "I helped with a business plan and projections so that she could apply at both the BDB and her own bank," recalls Dennis. "Probably Eva's strongest attribute is that she knows when she doesn't know what she's doing and she'll go out and hire the expertise she needs. Financing and accounting aren't her strong suit; that's why she came to us."

Dennis accompanied her to the bank to help her get the necessary loan (which she describes as having a "few zeros" to it). Eva presented the plan and did all the talking but relied on Dennis to

answer detailed financial questions. "For sure it makes a difference," says Dennis. "It makes the client a little more at ease and it
gives the banker a source of answers." Still, he believes Eva would
have got the money regardless, since her business plan was sound
and low-risk. After all, he points out, "She's providing a service in
an industry that's growing like a weed."

Indeed, Vancouver security companies reported growth of up
to 20 percent in 1996 as Vancouver reeled from increasing property-
crime rates that were more than double those of Toronto or
Montreal. Security concerns, coupled with new technological ways
to monitor just about anything, anywhere, result in a robust security industry. And in such a climate, Tricom faces increased competition from bigger companies, although it is still the only firm to
offer non-competitive monitoring.

In 1996, for example, the Rogers Commmunications Group of
Companies aggressively entered the B.C. market with Rogers
CanGuard Inc., which bought out Tricom's principal competitor,
Metropol Emergency Response Centre. For House, whose slogan,
"the leading edge," has always represented her commitment to the
latest in alarm-monitoring technology, competition from Rogers,
with its new two-way cable technology available for every home and
business, may eventually pose a high-tech threat. Still, neither
Vaughn Dennis nor one of her clients, Tony Oljaca, vice-president
of Accurate Safe & Alarm Co., a thirty-year-old Vancouver firm, are
too concerned.

"The small corner store didn't get squeezed out because the
big box stores came along," says Dennis. "There are always going to
be those who like the personalized service." Oljaca concurs. "They
[CanGuard] will compete against the larger companies for the cheap
jobs," he says. "I haven't lost one job to them in the last year."

Dennis foresees good growth in Tricom's security guard operation but predicts that the first-aid division will probably remain
stable. Growth in the alarm-monitoring operation may slow down
somewhat, he predicts, but says, "You can always get customers if
you can provide the service — there's no reason she can't do it in
the States as well as Canada."

Ultimately, House would like to push her alarm-monitoring business into California, and she also has her eye on the satellite tracking of stolen vehicles. Both ideas, however, need more study, and she thinks, as well, that it's time to concentrate on streamlining her business after going through so much growth. She states, quite frankly, that the certification and the computer crash, which cost her $90,000 in overtime alone, have hurt her business and cost her some clients. "I have to pull back and make sure that whichever route I take, it's not going to hurt the business in any way."

So for now, Eva House is counting on Tricom's impartiality, its reputation for excellent customer service, and its new, high-tech station and equipment to help her maintain her market leadership. "Keeping my competitive edge," she says, "is this year's big challenge."

WEN-DIZING **THE WEST**

DIANA JOSEPH

By Jane Harris

BOB HEWITT

" I knew in my thirties that was going to be my decade of accomplishment. I always knew I was going to run my own business. I just wasn't sure what it was going to be," says Calgarian Diana Joseph, thirty-seven, president and founder of Wen-Di Interiors. Joseph branched out on her own in 1986 and, today, her interior design company, which began as a home-based business, has eight branch offices throughout Alberta and British Columbia. It also has retail showrooms in Calgary, Edmonton, Kelowna, and Vancouver.

Each year, the company serves 4,200 clients and company files now contain records for 20,000 clients. Her 1997 sales target is $6 million and she expects to gross between 6 and 10 percent profit. Joseph has already taken Wen-Di Interiors through a financial crisis in the early 1990s, but her company emerged with a solid financial picture and management structure. Joseph also won a 1996 Canadian Woman Entrepreneur of the Year Award for her achievements.

Enter Wen-Di Interiors head office and showroom at 6170 12 Street SE, Calgary. As Joseph puts it, "It's fun. It's inviting. It inspires." The walls are rich forest green. Floral printed drapes hang from ornate golden rods throughout the room.

Diana Joseph steps into the showroom. She shows no hint of vulnerability and no one would guess she has two chronic illnesses.

Her hair is clipped short and her conservative green business suit is hemmed just above the knee. She wears almost no make-up, but her light brown hair is highlighted with golden blonde. I see glints of humour and sensitivity in her eyes.

Joseph's office is tucked away in a corner, at the right side of the building. In contrast to the opulent greens and golds that adorn the showroom, Joseph's office has white walls and few frills. Papers are scattered across the laminated desk. A row of family photos line the top of a cabinet.

I ask Joseph to describe herself. "Very driven, very goal-oriented," she says, "but I like to enjoy life." She won't tell me how much salary she takes home. She will say that she considers her lifestyle upper middle class. "I don't suffer," she says. Joseph quickly adds that the health of her company takes priority over her own comfort. She cut her salary to $100 a month plus child-care expenses when tough times hit in 1991 and says that her salary would be one of first she would cut if Wen-Di Interiors faced another financial crisis. "I didn't take anything for the first year and a half," she adds.

Wen-Di Interiors is growing faster than at any time since between the company's early growth years (1988–91). Joseph cites the company's increasing reputation, as well as a more buoyant economy in Calgary as explanations for her company's 70 percent rate of sales growth in 1996. "We still advertise," says Joseph. But the marketing budget is not as large as it used to be. "We have all our clients working out there for us," she says. Wen-Di implemented the Wen-Di Winner's Circle about a year ago. It gives customers points when they make purchases and refer new customers to Wen-Di Interiors. The sign-up fee is $10 and Circle members can also take free decorating seminars and get advance notice of promotions.

Joseph has seen a lot of competitors go bankrupt and, while her goal is to make Wen-Di Interiors a national company within ten years, she won't push the growth. "We've kind of explored the franchise — it's not our priority for the next while," says Joseph. Instead, the company is looking at setting up agency-based branch offices. The new agencies will be primarily owned by Wen-Di Interiors, but agents will own part of their own offices. "I do know, as much as I love what we do — the creative side — you have to run it as a business and educate yourself about business. You have to have a business plan or strategy. It's the hardest thing for a new business to do, but you have to do it. You have to get those dreams on paper — create some fact, not fantasy."

The company now has more than thirty employees. Joseph adds that only employees who have a degree or college diploma in Interior Design are allowed to call themselves designers. "We can tell pretty quickly if someone is just a sales person or has decorating ability."

Joseph believes in rewarding employees for their loyalty and contribution to the company. Wen-Di management also receive salaries, profit sharing, and bonuses. She has found that paying qualified people what they're worth has become a major, but necessary, expense. Her biggest expense, though, is keeping the thousands of product samples she needs to have on hand to show customers.

Although some things never go out of fashion, some decorating styles change quickly. "It used to be that styles changed only once every seven years but now two and a half to five years is the time for a change," says Joseph.

The average project rings in at about $1,500. Because individual home owners account for 70 percent of Wen-Di Interiors' sales, Joseph specializes in helping those who do not have unlimited budgets, skills, and energy — those who are neither do-it-yourselfers nor high-end design customers. Wen-Di Interiors serves its clients through its retail showrooms and in-home shopping. "We prefer to start at a client's home to get a better assessment of their lifestyle," explains Joseph.

Today, many national department stores who used to be Wen-Di Interiors' competition have moved to kiosks, subcontracting their decorating departments to other companies who rent space. On the other end, big box stores offer one-stop shopping for do-it-yourselfers. Joseph is not worried about competition. "Because of our positioning, there's minor overlap," she says. Still, both big box stores and smaller retailers offer some of the services she does, and Joseph is also ready to help both the high-end customer and the do-it-yourself enthusiast. "We don't turn a customer away, that's for sure," she adds.

"She believes in giving people more than they expect to get," says Heather Hill, who works at Hunter Douglas Window Fashions in Edmonton. Hill knows she can count on Joseph to call and relay her concerns point by point when service needs to be improved. She adds that Joseph is no more demanding of others than she is of herself.

Diana's father, Al Westman, says that his daughter worked hard at things that did not come easily to her — like skiing — until she excelled. Joseph remembers learning to ski, too. "All three of us kids decided we wanted skiing lessons," she says. "In those days, you put out your arm and the size of the ski you got was the length of your arm. So, we go off with the ski instructor. Everybody else takes to it like ducks to water. I was a tangled mess. My ski instructor just left me on the hill all afternoon. I was laughed at and ridiculed." Joseph spent many more afternoons tangled up on the hill, but she kept asking her parents to take her back. "I had something to prove," she says. "I became the best skier in the family."

"If Diana wants to do something, she finds a way to do it," says her mother, Bev Westman, who remembers nine-year-old Diana and a friend participating in a twenty-five-mile walk-a-thon. "You know those two girls completed it. Her feet were in horrible shape. She couldn't walk to pick up her pledges," remembers Westman.

Diana was in such a rush to be born, says Westman, that he and Bev delivered her themselves and called the doctor later. When the doctor arrived and asked for string to cut the cord, "my husband came out with Christmas ribbon," Bev adds. Diana has an older brother, Jay, thirty-eight, and a younger sister, Janet, thirty-three. "There's always rivalry between the three of them," says Diana's husband, Ken Joseph. "With her brother, it's usually all business. They can't wait to get together so they can talk about business. The whole world stops while they solve problems."

After graduating from Dr. E.P. Scarlett High School in Calgary in 1978, Joseph went straight into the work force. "I didn't know what I wanted to do in university," she explains. "In high school, I held down a couple of jobs and I really enjoyed it. I wanted to start making my mark." She became first a junior accountant, then head of accounting at an automotive business. "I didn't know I didn't like accounting — it was a good opportunity with a good company," she says. Surprisingly, she adds that her talents do not really lie in interior design, either — "I have more talented people doing that."

Diana says she started her own interior design business because the opportunity presented itself. But she adds that if she hadn't gone into the decorating business, she would have found something else. She considers herself to be a marketer and a leader.

At age twenty, she met Ken Joseph, a school teacher eleven years older than she was. He was newly divorced and teaching school in Wildwood, Alberta, a small town northeast of Edmonton. The two were married on October 10, 1981, after only ten months of long-distance dating. "We didn't even know each other when we got engaged and we'd spent about twelve days together," Diana remembers. She pauses. "I got lucky," she adds. "I wouldn't recommend others to do that."

Ken Joseph remains an anchor in Diana's life. "I knew there was a lot of drive when I married her — it's one of the reasons for [marrying her]," he says. Ken adds that he knew his future wife was forthright and determined early in their relationship. She took him aside and asked, "So, where's this relationship going?" He decided to propose marriage right away.

At twenty-three, Joseph became pregnant and bolted from the job market. "I had a good position, but I thought I'd try this motherhood thing," she says. Her daughter, Sarah, was often sick and gained very little weight.

"They were pinpointing the problem on me, saying it was due to lack of bonding — and was psychological on my end. I believed them," she says. Health professionals said the underweight baby needed more milk. Joseph followed their advice and forced forty ounces of milk into her child daily. The baby continued to cry for hours on end. At eighteen months, after an exhausted Joseph had dissolved into tears in the doctor's office, Sarah was diagnosed with severe milk allergies. "I was begging for help and didn't know how to tell people to help," says Joseph.

"I knew at that point, for my sanity and my self-confidence, I had to get back out working," says Joseph. "I didn't feel challenged enough, and I also did not like not having my own income." At first, Joseph hoped to find a place in her father's business.

Her brother, Jay, had gone to work with their father, a land developer, while he was still in his late teens. But, by 1981, the family company was in receivership. "It was a combination of the oil bust and the bank's high interest rates of 22 to 23 percent. We couldn't pay these high interest rates. Calgary was a disaster at that time," remembers Beverly Westman.

Her father's receivership didn't dampen Diana's enthusiasm for entrepreneurship. "He handled it in such a way that we were upset, but it was better for us. It required us to stand on our own even more. We were used to having an affluent lifestyle." It also meant that Diana would have to carve out her own business from scratch.

Her father and brother picked themselves up and started over. In 1983, Diana hoped that she might become a part of the new family enterprise, Jayman Master Builders. She asked Al and Jay for a job — but they said no. "I didn't really have any skills — didn't have education in marketing," says Joseph.

Jay and Al tried to create a role for her. They asked Joseph and Jay's wife, Wendy, to start decorating show homes. "They had us do the stereotype basically. You know, keep the little sister happy." The work was sporadic and it wasn't full-time but "it became pretty evident that I wasn't satisfied with that. We made a little money," says Joseph.

In a year or two, Joseph realized the concept could be improved and that she could become a full-service decorator with a capacity to tap the retail market. Wendy did not want to go into business full-time.

In 1986, the pair split the $1,000 they had in their joint busi-
ness account and Joseph proceeded to build her own company.
She decided to keep the name Wen-Di Interiors. "We had a little
name recognition and I couldn't come up with another name I
liked," she explains.

Joseph's first trip to the banker in search of financing for her
new venture was a disaster. After slaving over a detailed business
plan (with help of an accountant friend) that included high, me-
dium, and low sales projections, she was ready to put her plan into
action. She brought the banker her plan, an optimistic outlook,
and a request — for a $5,000 line of credit and $5,000 loan.

"He never even looked at my business plan," she remembers.
Instead, the banker spent an hour and a half asking Joseph how
her husband felt about the business and why he was not involved in
it. She already had her own work history and credit rating — and
she didn't want her husband's signature on her loan. She left angry
but not defeated. Next, she visited a female banker at the Royal
Bank and got a loan in ten minutes. Joseph has stayed with the
Royal Bank ever since.

Acquaintances still occasionally express surprise that Joseph has
her own office. She has, at times, been viewed as the daughter of a
builder rather than the founder of a thriving business. Joseph knows
she's fighting stereotypes and that she is lucky to have the chance
to build her own business. "There still are not a lot of women in
high-profile positions in general," she adds. "Our mothers were not
necessarily given that opportunity. I was also fighting youth and
certain preconceptions working with builders and clients in a male-
dominated industry. I had to mature through the process. At twenty-
five, I was fairly mature, but not in business ways."

Joseph has had no female business mentors. It was her father
who coached her. "My dad grew up in the Depression. A lot of
people didn't finish high school, it was just kind of expected to get
to Grade 8 or 9 and they went out and worked," she says. She says
her father has "real good common sense" and strong values —
such as if you shake hands, you make a deal. "That's the way it is.
You can do the paperwork later, " says Joseph, who has adopted her

father's business values. "She is very sensitive when she says people should take her at her word," says Ken Joseph."She goes out of her way to make sure it's a fair deal."

In the early days, her father would sometimes pull her aside going out of a meeting. He would tell her which dress was not appropriate, when to be quiet, how to deal with bankers. She says she had to learn that, in business, "there are ways to act and ways not to act."

Al and Jay sometimes viewed Diana's concerns as family issues — not business ones. For example, her father taught her to pay all her suppliers immediately. "The only person they didn't pay," she says, "was me." She adds that, when the office got busy, it was easier for Jayman to delay checking her invoices and writing her a cheque because she was a family member. In late 1986, Diana invoiced Jayman $750 for late payment. "After that, we never had a problem," she says. "They'd never let money separate the family, but you have to earn the respect to do business with them," say Joseph. "You have to work even harder." Joseph has earned her father's respect. "She's a lot smarter, no question," Al Westman adds. "She listens and weighs all the angles."

Joseph believes her company is more resilient because she has learned to ask for help."We're continually educating ourselves and our management team. We know that we don't know it all — and ask for help, " she explains. Joseph adds that business is changing so quickly, it's almost impossible to keep up." She loves to read as many as six business books in one weekend and gets her staff to read the ones she likes. She also "Wen-Dizes" all her employees by providing in-house training in corporate culture and customer service. "I'm a big proponent of education, even though I don't have [much] formally. I am continually educating myself," she says. She and her staff do regular strategic planning and competitive analysis, focusing on the company's strengths and weakness. She concentrates on global and national trends while her managers do regional analysis.

"I'm basically on a plane every eight days," she says. Her trips last from two days to a week and a half as she travels across North

America to meet with suppliers, visit trade shows, and compare notes with other business people. She loves to travel but has mixed feelings about leaving her husband and children at home. "About the second day, I miss them very badly — then I get preoccupied." She also feels guilty about leaving so much family responsibility on her husband's shoulders. "He's been a single parent and that's a heavy load," she admits. Ken takes a more casual attitude about the workload at home — "Generally when she needs to be doing her stuff, I just pick up the slack at home. It's not a big issue."

Joseph watches every division, trying to make it pay for itself within a couple of years. To accomplish her goals, she will change management, marketing, or her sales approach. "If an employee or division is not creating profit, we look to guide them in a different direction — working with them, being honest with them, and looking for creative solutions together," she explains. Wen-Di Interiors has three criteria for dismissal: not providing customer satisfaction, inability to be a team player, and missing sales quotas. Firings are a last resort, though. "But you can't always be loved," says Joseph. She says she is learning to hire better and cut the cord more quickly. Usually she can tell within three months whether an employee will fit into her business.

In 1991, Joseph strategically planned the birth of her second child to coincide with the expansion of her business. Much to her doctor's amazement, Joseph successfully engineered her son's birthday to occur near the end of the school year. In addition to his paternity leave, Ken Joseph was able to care for the baby during his summer off from teaching school. Their son, Weston, was born on the Tuesday after the Victoria Day weekend, and Diana was back in her office part-time by Friday.

By the time Weston was six months old, Diana was facing a financial crisis. Looking back, Joseph says she was trying to push a market — the consumer market — that wasn't there. Between 1988 and 1991, the company's early success had kept it growing and Joseph was confident the growth would continue. She moved to her current location, a strip mall where her showroom samples could be better displayed, and became involved in a joint venture with a carpet company in Edmonton, where she wanted to expand her operations. She borrowed money to finance the expansion, and the higher overhead meant she had to increase sales to make a profit. But Wen-Di never achieved its projected sales.

At first, the red ink upset Joseph. She was used to seeing profit on her company's income statements. Then she began listening to people who told her not to worry about the debt. She started playing games with herself about the sales figures she was seeing month after month. "We're so close," she'd say. "It's just around the corner."

Joseph faced the truth after she visited a banker — not her own — who looked at her figures and told her the company was in trouble. She was angry, not just with the banker, but with herself. "I created an atmosphere where yes people were the only people who could be around me," she explains.

She and her staff sat down as a team to deal with the crisis. "It was a good way to find out who was onside and who wasn't," she says. She asked staff to chip money into the coffee fund. All but one employee co-operated. On her way to a lunch, Joseph crunched up the car she was driving — she was venting her frustration about the coffee fund and forgot to pay attention to the road. "It was awful, and, of course, my husband was upset because he loved that car. I had a headache. I really wanted to run away that night."

Human casualties were minimal — one layoff, one firing (over the coffee fund), and the dissolution of the joint venture with the carpet company. "Both of us took a kicking," says Joseph. "They [still] have a strong working relationship with us. But it was tough. I was lucky. I didn't have to [cash in RRSPs] or liquidate my personal assets," says Joseph. She had never taken large chunks of equity out of her company and by reducing her salary, cutting expenses, and restructuring the company, she kept her own banker's goodwill. "I got proactive before they got nasty," she says.

She pared company expenses to a minimum, cancelled a vacation, and paid herself $100 a month plus child-care expenses. She also liquefied stocks and paid off her personal line of credit. "I had to retain shareholder's equity. The bank restricted the amount I could pull from the company," she says. That meant Joseph had to do some things she had always avoided doing. She had to have her husband sign her personal guarantee, which rose from $40,000 to $90,000, and she was not allowed to pay back her father money she borrowed to finance the dissolution of the joint venture until after her finances were put back in order.

"We never missed a payment," says Joseph. But nine months later, when Weston was only eighteen months old, she was still seeing red ink. Ready to quit, she had a conversation with her father, telling him that she was not fighting any more and her new goal was to get ready to sell Wen-Di Interiors. "I was defeated and exhausted," says Joseph. Al told her the crisis was over, but Joseph was sceptical. "Three or four weeks later we made money, one month, the next month.... It was over. He could see it, I couldn't," says Joseph. Al Westman puts it this way: "We just reassured her of it. I wouldn't let her quit. I just wouldn't let her quit."

No sooner did Joseph have her business under control than an even bigger crisis loomed. She was diagnosed with fibromyalgia in December 1994. Fibromyalgia affects the muscles and tissues and is escalated by stress. "Pain in different parts of the body can translate into all-over pain," says Joseph. "It feels like a truck hit you." Aside from the pain, its by-product is constant fatigue. "I didn't feel like I could get through the day. My fatigue was so strong. I'd eat supper and I'd have to go to bed. I couldn't stay awake. You just think you're tired and everybody's tired, aren't they? You don't want to complain about it." She adds, "I never understood why women who found breast lumps would delay going to the doctor. I understand that now." Ken finally forced her to see a doctor. "It just seemed to be the woman's disease of the nineties," she says. "I was very worried about our major clients — in the building and builder community — because, first off, it's a woman's illness and I was worried that if they even thought there was any vulnerability we would start losing accounts," says Joseph.

She hired two consultants and a human resources person. "They rearranged everything in the company so it wasn't running around me any more," Joseph remembers. She had wanted to make changes in her company prior to her diagnosis. "Now I didn't have a choice," she says. She tells other entrepreneurs, "We like to know that we have all the answers. But we're always vulnerable if we retain complete control of day-to-day operations of the company. If we die, the company becomes insolvent." These days, Wen-Di Interiors is managed with a lot more paper, detail, and cold hard facts.

Joseph moved to a less than half-time schedule. "I would go to the Okanagan every three weeks to rest for three or four days. I could go home, but I still felt guilty. The household help didn't understand why I was lying in bed," she says.

In October 1995, less than a year after the first diagnosis, she began noticing a tingling sensation in her legs and her legs giving out. This time, she did not wait to get help. Her doctor soon told her that, in addition to fibromyalgia, she had multiple sclerosis. She had watched her maternal grandmother, Lois Gillespie, struggle with M.S. for years before she died in 1989. "I watched her body give out and she never complained," says Joseph. Gillespie remains Joseph's hero. "I always knew she was there for me. She always believed in me and was extremely positive."

Again, Joseph felt vulnerable. She knew that she could lose her major accounts and she could become too ill to work. "In my mind, it showed a sign of weakness. I had to have a game plan in place." She decided that since she was ill, she needed a stronger company. She cut back on her own work load, but she did not downsize Wen-Di Interiors. She set goals to restructure the company and move it towards more financial stability and less dependence upon her being there. "It was the best thing that could have happened to the company," she says.

As far as dealing with the medical system, she says, "You have to get aggressive in a couple of different ways. You have to educate yourself, you have to ask a lot of questions." She found that unless she could specifically define her symptoms and compare them to something else, doctors didn't always understand what she was telling them.

Joseph used to have a mainstream approach to her own health care. She now believes there is room for both alternative and mainstream medicine, but remains sceptical about the qualifications of some of those practising alternative treatments. "I only go to people with education and specific skills," she says. She sees a naturopath, who prescribes supplements to "enhance components of her system," in addition to her family doctor. She also continues to treat her illnesses with pacing and self-care.

Joseph used to work twelve- to fourteen-hour days. "I was never home till the kids were in bed." She says Ken wasn't happy, but he was good about it. "After a while, over time, they come to get used to it," she says. She cut her hours of work to less than half-time for a while after she got sick, but her old work habits have already started creeping back. "In the last four months, it's gotten to that level again. Basically, it's because of moving the company to the next level [of growth]," says Joseph.

When she's tempted to work too hard, she says Ken reminds her of her priorities and helps her keep her balance. Family remains extremely important to Joseph.

The big family meal on Sundays often includes her parents and her brother's family. She tries to spend as much time as possible with Sarah and Weston and Weston loves having his mom volunteer in his kindergarten class. "She puts work aside. She tries to be there," says Ken.

Joseph says, "It's just a matter of finding the right thing that you love." Her own success has come with some hard lessons, long hours, and tough choices. It's the rewards and Diana's own determination that spur her on. Money, she says, is only a by-product. "I like the freedom," she explains. "When I want to take a day off, I can. I like the challenge and it's always a learning environment."

15 SEEING IS BELIEVING

DOROTHY SPENCE
AND LINDA WEAVER

By Margo Brunelle

When Ryan Fudge was twelve years old, his badly congested lungs were plastered all over the TV news. Not a pretty picture, but it captured a lot of attention! They were the first organs to be X-rayed in one part of the Maritimes and examined within moments on a computer screen two and a half hours away — by car and ferry. Ryan lives on Grand Manan Island, in the mouth of the Bay of Fundy. His lungs were seen by a radiologist who works at Saint John Regional Hospital, Saint John, New Brunswick. It was the first, but not the last, time the two met through a magical link-up called telemedicine.

Telemedicine is not new to Canada, but most of us haven't heard of it yet or realized the impact it could have on our lives. Ryan, for instance, was saved the agony of an emergency trip to Saint John — or, at the very least, was spared the stress of waiting nearly two weeks to find out why he could barely breathe. It used to take about that long for X-rays to be delivered to Saint John, interpreted by a radiologist, and a full report returned by road and ferry. Using telemedicine, Ryan immediately got the diagnosis and antibiotics he needed.

Another name for telemedicine is distance medicine because it links patients and clinicians who are in different locations. Sometimes their interaction does not require pictures — and in those cases, the telephone still works well. But in a modern age when the delivery of health care is restricted by cost, travel, and the availability of clinical services, the world of medicine is ripe for innovation.

Enter the TecKnowledge team. Dorothy Spence and Linda Weaver are innovators and integraters. Using video images and audio, they have found ways to extend specialized health-care services to remote parts of the world. No roads are needed, just the Information Highway. Spence and Weaver hit *that* road two years ago, and already they are miles ahead of other international companies selling telemedicine technology.

The president and CEO of TecKnowledge, Dorothy Spence, sits across a broad expanse of desk and beams at the distance they've covered and the view that lies ahead. She relishes reliving the frustrating moments because she knows there's a happy ending in sight. "People say, 'Oh you're *so successful.*'" She does a mock double-take and breaks into giggles. "Are you talking to *me?*"

It was only a couple of years ago that TecKnowledge was holed up in the basement of Linda Weaver's suburban home, operating on a $50,000 line of credit. In 1996, the company wrapped up a fiscal year with more than $4 million in sales, and the contracts keep getting bigger. These days TecKnowledge is chasing multi-million-dollar projects — and it's all been accomplished in a very short time.

For someone who's sitting on the edge of a burgeoning empire, Dorothy Spence shows none of the pretensions of success. At the age of thirty-five, she's an inspiring blend of schemer and dreamer. Her dark eyes flash and twinkle, but they never waver from their focus. For all her energy and spirit, Spence does not lose control of her ways and words. "Linda and I have always been business colleagues — I guess we're friends!" she adds, laughing cautiously.

Spence and Weaver met in 1982, when they were studying engineering at the Technical University of Nova Scotia. In their spare time, they played volleyball with the women's varsity team. (Spence says the games she's played have taught her a lot about endurance, perseverance, and competition.)

"We don't hang out together, but I recognized that working together we were a very powerful team. We were always creating new programs ... and innovating, and really pushing our projects in a different direction."

This project has taken them in a direction they did not map out. Spence finished her mechanical engineering degree, but admits she's surprised when she sees that iron ring on her finger. She is the marketing and business brain on the TecKnowledge team. Her bright and comfortable office conspicuously lacks the technology that consumes her life.

Waving her hand at a desktop computer beside her, she confesses, "I know it's a computer — but that's about all!" Clearly, Weaver is the technical wizard at TecKnowledge Healthcare Sytems, Inc.

Linda Weaver, thirty-seven, looks like a mom you might run into at the playground with her kids — a little dishevelled, with warm, worried eyes that wander as if she's always thinking about the groceries, ballet lessons, a load of laundry she left in the washing machine. Of course, she's many miles from household chores, but her mind is an endless list of small details and big responsibilities.

"Dorothy and I are a very different kettle of fish," Weaver acknowledges. "She's like a bull in a china shop! She sees something and goes for it. I'm much more the collect and gather, collect and gather mode. We annoy each other mutually because we have very different skills."

What they have in common is some early experience as clinical engineers — explaining and evaluating high-tech equipment to sceptical physicians.

After finishing engineering degrees (and in Linda's case, some handy computer courses), they both worked for the Nova Scotia Association of Health Organizations (NSAHO), a non-profit outfit that provides advice, support, and expertise to health-care facilities in Nova Scotia.

Dorothy was naturally drawn into health care — her mother is a nurse, and several siblings, including a brother, are nurses. But

Linda had graduated as an electrical engineer and ended up with NSAHO under a hiring program for women in non-traditional fields. Spence stayed four years, and Weaver five, and during that time they learned about the practical application of health-care technology. Today, their company is known for its unique approach to telemedicine, because they customize and evaluate their equipment to meet specific clinical needs. Health-care clinicians can be cautious, conservative, and sometimes resistant to new technology. Spence and Weaver realize their most important job is to get the users onside so that no one ends up with a hunk of useless and expensive machinery.

Weaver, chief technical officer and chair of the board, occupies a cramped office several floors under Spencer, in the bowels of a building owned by Maritime Medical Care (a company that runs Nova Scotia's health insurance plan, and sells private health insurance). It's a pink concrete low-rise, nestled in trees on the edge of an otherwise barren industrial park. She shares the office with David Rilling, a technologist who designs hardware, and a confusing stash of computer components, cameras, and medical gizmos of various shapes and sizes.

"We knew we were going to butt heads," Weaver says as she explains her relationship with Dorothy, "but we discovered that when we came to some kind of consensus, it was always the best decision because we both have to make the other person understand what our point of view is."

"Marketing meets technology" sounds like the perfect equation — but this partnership sometimes seems more like a paradox. It's not that they don't have the same vision. Spence and Weaver tell me again and again that they "want to make a difference." Telemedicine is perhaps our last best option for a streamlined yet compassionate health-care system. But just as in a marriage, these two partners do not always agree about how to get "there" from "here." Marketing strategy is based on fast moves and the big picture. Technological innovation is gained through nitty-gritty problem solving. Spence and Weaver readily admit that sometimes the two collide with a loud crash. They like to call it "creative tension."

For a few years they went their separate ways in private industry. Dorothy strayed into sales and business management for Medi-Gas, a company that sold oxygen and anaesthetic equipment. She did remarkably well, considering she still "didn't have a clue" about business marketing. At the age of twenty-nine, she was given bottom-line responsibility for a $12-million corporation.

Linda, meanwhile, faced her own challenges in electrical engineering. She went to work for IOTEK, a defence-electronics research and development company involved in large-scale hardware/software integration projects. During this period both women built up some personal savings, which provided crucial cash flow in the years down the road.

Spence and Weaver kept in touch occasionally, and their paths crossed again in 1992 at St. Mary's University in Halifax. Tired of the corporate world, they had both decided to take graduate studies in business management, although by then they were wives and mothers. They decided to start an engineering consulting company, planning to use the experience and financial rewards to get them through the executive MBA program, a commitment of thirty hours a week. The business consumed fifty or sixty hours. The money was spare and sporadic. Luckily, the office — Linda's basement — was handy to at least one of them.

"I remember coming down (into Weaver's basement) one morning and seeing this line of dirty plates, and spoons, and forks and knives — and Linda, staring at the monitor, still typing." Like many women who set themselves up as consultants, hoping it will provide flexibility in their lives, Spence and Weaver discovered they were working around the clock for next to nothing, and worrying *all* the time.

When they finished their degrees, they knew they had to make a crucial career move. "Finding the business was an accident," offers Linda, "but I think we made the accident happen!" The "accident" was telemedicine.

They found it while doing research for a "value-added reseller," a telecommunications company that was looking for new ways to offer cheap packages to heavy long-distance users. In a highly competitive market, that company didn't last, but Spence and Weaver picked up where that research left off, realizing that the health-care sector could be a ready and willing customer for telemedicine applications.

"We didn't know anything about telemedicine when we started," admits Spence. "We hadn't even heard about it."

They started making calls and reading journals. It didn't take long to learn that the industry was going through explosive growth in the United States.

"We knew the technology diffusion rate in Canada is about two years behind the United States," Spence explains. "We don't accept or adopt technology as fast."

Weaver credits the environment she grew up in with giving her confidence to take advantage of opportunities. She is the oldest of three daughters. Her parents, both college-educated, had an entrepreneurial bent, too. By the time Linda was eight, Charles Weaver had taken his family from Seattle, Washington, to Kingston, Ontario, on to Brockville, then Fredericton, and still farther east to Stephenville, Newfoundland, in a quest to be his own boss. After trying aviation, financial management, and mineral processing, he now runs a marina in Baddeck, Cape Breton. Of course, Atlantic Canada is a place where people are blessed with the strength to believe in themselves against all odds. Linda had that message drilled into her as she grew up.

"Anytime anyone tried to restrict us, my parents got *in their face*," she recalls. "When my guidance counsellor told me to be a primary-school teacher, my mother had a long and loud discussion with her!"

While Charles Weaver was occcupied with his business pursuits, his wife kept things together at home — and in her spare time ran a jewellery franchise. Every night after supper and homework, the kids would help their mom tie tags on trinkets and pack boxes. The work ethic never let up. Tragically, when Linda was sixteen, her mother was killed in a car acccident. She had to take over raising her sisters.

Weaver now has two young children herself, but husband George Matthews, forty-one, is the anchor. A public-school teacher, he's taken extended leave from the chaos in the classroom to try to keep control at home. Meanwhile, Linda puts in about seventy hours a week for TecKnowledge. "I don't think he knew it would be this bad, but any job I've had I always worked fifty or sixty hours," she admits.

As the technical expert on the team, Weaver has spent many of those hours on the road, sometimes in cities, but also in far-flung communities that are cut off from quality health care. It's in those places that telemedicine has had the greatest impact. And although it's been lonely for Linda — endless hours spent under desks, hooking up the telemedicine computer station — it's also been a thrill to see the expressions on people's faces when they can finally watch "Joe, in the lab!" hundreds of miles away across inaccessible terrain. "You go through two weeks of hell, then two hours of watching how (telemedicine) impacts on them. It makes it all worthwhile."

She also makes several trips a year as Canadian president of the Institute of Electrical and Electronics Engineers (a learning experience for George, who's often expected to wear a pink name tag identifying him as the "spouse of ....").

In a phone conversation punctuated by hungry, tired kids, George Matthews confesses he worries about Linda, flying from one place to another, staying alone in strange cities. Their two-year-old, Timothy, can be heard whimpering at his dad's feet. He thinks it's his mom, calling home from far away.

Sometimes the whole family goes along for the ride. That's what they did when Linda had to fly to Washington for a telemedicine conference a few weeks after Timothy, their second child, was born. She would walk the floor of the showroom, sizing up the hardware and wheeling and dealing with sales people, then run up to her hotel room to breastfeed then phone Dorothy with wildly excited reports. It was a turning point for their company.

Linda had found the flexible, feasible "work station" they needed to tackle telemedicine full-speed. Within weeks, Dorothy was in a lawyer's office, listening to her husband, Dale, get "the goods" on using their mortgage as collateral.

It was a risk they weren't completely prepared for. After the Washington conference, Linda and Dorothy tackled the first bank they could think of — the Credit Union Atlantic, where Linda had got a loan previously and was still grateful.

"Picture this — we walk in, introduce ourselves, and announce that we have all this knowledge and a *wonderful* idea," Dorothy recounts without a hint of embarrassment or bitterness. "But no assets!"

Now she really has a good laugh. "What do you think the response was?"

Dorothy has never been afraid of a challenge and has a good stomach for risk taking. She is the middle child of five, born in Montreal to Irish-French parents. Her father worked in industrial sales for Acme Steel and moved the family to northern New Brunswick when Dorothy was ten. Perhaps because of her place in the birth order she says she has a competitive edge on most of her siblings. They still tease her about the claim she made one day as a kid, listening to an Anne Murray song on the car radio. "When I grow up I'm going to be filthy rich like her!" she boasted.

After their first humiliation, Spence and Weaver didn't waste time hounding other doubtful bankers. They simply turned to their husbands for the personal guarantees they needed.

"There's a number of times when things are *seared* into an entrepreneur's brain, making them even more determined to succeed!" Spence recounts. "That was one of them, because Dale was really nervous and turned to me and said, 'I must *really* love you.'"

During a few minutes of quiet at home, Dale proudly flips through photos of their travels — Dorothy cavorting with a kangaroo, on a long sojourn through the South Pacific. Later, with their two children, two-year-old Laura and infant Mitchell in tow, they took off to Europe for two months during her maternity leave.

"And when we got back, Dorothy was counting pennies for groceries on the kitchen table," he laughs. "It was her idea completely. She spurs us on!"

Spurred on by a computer supplier in Massachusetts and $50,000 in the bank, Spence and Weaver felt ready to conquer the world. But the Information Highway has some unexpected twists and potholes.

Spence is energetic and stubborn, but even she nearly succumbed to the stress of that first year, when they had given up all their extra contract work to focus exclusively on telemedicine. Their line of credit ran out, and the bills for phone, rent, and office furniture poured in.

Fortunately, each offered the other support and encouragement in tough times. But there were moments of real despair when Dorothy had to look up her "official mentor" for inspiration. Grace White, "another feisty female entrepreneur," is president of Can-Jam Trading Ltd., a company she started from home, exporting food products first to the Caribbean, now all over the world. In 1993 she was Canadian Woman Entrepreneur of the Year for International Competitiveness, and when Dorothy Spence came calling, White was well-equipped to dish up some valuable advice. "Never mind the cash crisis. If you believe in what you're doing, you'll figure out a way to do it."

Dorothy says, "So I came back to the office, and I said, 'Linda! We got it all wrong! We thought you had to see in order to believe. You gotta believe in order to see!'"

Their first order came in the next week. It was a contract with Health Canada, to hook up two remote nursing stations in northern Ontario with Sioux Lookout, the consulting site. Their second contract linked Ryan Fudge on Grand Manan to Saint John Regional Hospital on "the mainland." Those two deals taught them a lot about the theory of relativity as it applies to the world of high tech.

"Telemedicine is full of what we call *vapour,*" Dorothy explains. "Things you think exist don't really. And businesses you think are big aren't — because that's not the stage the industry is in."

Spence and Weaver seem to be far from "vapour." They are unpretentious and pragmatic. It was precisely those qualities that helped them choose a product that is relatively simple (and ultimately useful). They've been so busy selling and installing, they haven't even come up with a name for it. But the idea of a telehealth work station is winning solid support with clinicians, patients, and politicians. Clinicians like it because it saves time. Patients like it because it saves stress. Politicians like it because it could save precious health-care dollars and solve the problem of how to get doctors to serve rural areas.

Each work station is just a normal computer with a Windows interface and special devices added on: an electronic stethoscope, a blood pressure machine, a microscope with a camera attached for pathology slides, an electro-cardiograph (EKG) to transmit heart signals, otoscopes for ear, nose, and throat, and perhaps most important, the X-ray machine and ultrasound for transmitting images within minutes.

These tools are connected to the computer through an audio channel or video source; the remote site (where a nurse or X-ray technician is stationed) is linked to the consulting site (where a specialist makes the diagnosis) using a modem. In its simplest form, it allows medical professionals and patients or their families to consult with each other in real time, using video-conferencing. When the proper connections are made, it allows a sick person at a clinic in the wilderness to be examined by a top-quality specialist anywhere in the world.

Of course, the proper connections are not always easy to make. One of the frustrations that Spence and Weaver have had to confront is the discrepancy in telecommunications from one part of the country to another. The better the technology, the clearer the video images they are able to transmit via telemedicine.

"The more remote the location, the more determined we are to get there," Dorothy explains. "But the more remote the location, the worse the telecommunications." It's a conundrum that will take their most persuasive powers to resolve.

If Spence and Weaver have any "tough sells," it won't be with the parents of sick children who travel to Halifax from all over the region for specialized care. After a year or so in second gear, their business suddenly went into overdrive in January 1996, when they got the nod from Ruby Blois, at the IWK-Grace Health Centre in Halifax.

A nurse with thirty years' experience under her cap, Blois is now director of Partnership Development at the the referral hospital for children and maternity patients in the Maritimes. She has the same forward-thinking business smarts as Spence and Weaver. Together, they spearheaded a unique partnership called the Children's Tele-Health Project, which links the IWK-Grace with three general hospitals in the region.

It's a breakthrough for telemedicine — the first multi-site link-up in the world. Not surprisingly, it's been a steep learning curve for the TecKnowledge team.

"They're tough-minded about doing things right, but very, very patient," acknowledges Blois.

They have had to be. Physicians are, by necessity, perfectionists. Not all of them have been satisfied with the quality of the technology yet.

"I can say clearly, in terms of value, what our costs were and what they've contributed in developmental time — they haven't made money on this one!" Blois admits.

Each hospital has bought one work station at a cost of $100,000. Blois foresees a day when every physician will have a work station right in his or her office and links with a dozen or more hospitals around the region, saving the health-care system about $8,000 for every air transport not required.

In the meantime, telemedicine technology continues to blossom, and Weaver travels the world looking for creative applications. She claims there is no limit to the possibilities.

"We are poised on the edge of something that's just going to explode," she boasts matter-of-factly. But she catches her breath. "We look at where we were eighteen months ago, and it's amazing. How the hell did we do that? And then we think, where are we going to be in a year or two?"

They have gone from their first office (the one in the basement of Linda's home), to their first real office (in a warehouse, since demolished), to their first downtown office (now being renovated to remove asbestos), to their first official office, in partnership with Maritime Medical Care, Limited.

As Dorothy takes me on a tour, she stops to gaze longingly through the glass doors of an office right off the main lobby. She is pining to move in — to assemble her own team all in one place and to decorate it with medical artifacts and curios. In the meantime, TecKnowledge is crammed into crowded offices all over the building. It's a good thing this company specializes in remote communication.

TecKnowledge reached a second turn in the road about four months after their big sale to IWK-Grace. The business was attracting more interest than Weaver and Spence could handle. The $50,000 cash flow was a pittance in a high-tech marketplace, so they used personal savings, RRSPs, and their husbands' incomes to fill the gap. Their supplier was unreliable. And Linda was still doing all the installations herself. Even with a million dollars' worth of sales booked, bankruptcy was a threat. The two women needed help; they needed a reliable cash flow, business contacts, and a support staff.

"I met Jim Moir [president and CEO of Maritime Medical Care] at a talk he gave on psychology and motivation to our executive MBA class," Dorothy recalls. "But I was the only one in the class who made an appointment to see him afterwards. I said [to Moir], 'I'm here to tell you a story of courage and human spirit. I'm going to tell you about two courageous women!'" Moir listened to Dorothy's story, and a year later, in April 1996, his company bought a 50 percent equity in TecKnowledge.

Both sides are loath to reveal the selling price, although Linda has let it slip that it was a six-figure sum. Whatever the exact price, all parties agree it's the perfect marriage. Moir, who is a director but not an active member of the TecKnowledge team, offers the voice of reason, experience, and inspiration to a fast-growing company. Maritime Medical Care provides the technical support, financial backing, and credibility Spence and Weaver desperately needed. And TecKnowledge gives Maritime Medical Care a great new business opportunity.

The deal also relieved the pressures on Spence and Weaver and their families. The personal hardships have let up. Their work week is somewhat more manageable, and at last they have some money in the bank.

Spence says she's stopped looking at price tags, has started swimming three times a week, is catching up on sleep, and gave up coffee and wine as comforts at the end of a long day.

Both women acknowledge they could never have got this far without husbands who are exceptionally supportive and willing to fill the gap at home. But this is where the partnership arrives at a fork in the road.

Spence confesses she lives from vacation to vacation. Her dream is to get the company rolling smoothly, work thirty-five hours a week, and make lots of money. But Spence says Weaver "wants to save the world." Weaver manages to get by on five hours' sleep, no exercise, and little fresh air. She wants to work for twenty or thirty years and face lots of big, new challenges in that time. This is the life she and her family have always known. She's committed and *fairly* content with it.

As contracts add up, so does their confidence. In the early days, Spence confesses they made the mistake of blaming themselves for everything that went wrong, including the supplier who didn't deliver on promises. Now they are assembling more rugged and powerful work stations themselves.

They have negotiated deals from the Middle East to the Caribbean and have won interest in the United States, too (although there the health-care system is so fragmented that link-ups are more complicated, and telemedicine has been slower to catch on). Spence and Weaver are convinced that TecKnowledge is the only company in the world offering a full range of telemedicine products and services, designed by clinical engineers.

And how do clients react to two women from the Maritimes in a highly competitive, developmental field? "Well, if you think it's a strike against you, it becomes a strike against you," Dorothy argues. "So I normally start out my conversation, 'You may think we're a small Maritime company, or even *just* a Canadian company but we're into total global domination' — and we keep reminding them of that!" Both acknowledge they've run up against some silly and some serious sexism over the years. But they refuse to dwell on those experiences. They prefer to believe they are stronger and more determined to succeed because of it.

Dorothy and Linda are nothing like the chic, glamorous businesswomen who are often held up as role models in glossy magazines. Their sense of self-worth goes much deeper than that because their success is based on knowledge, not image. Dorothy's feminist spirit was honed at a tender age, when a guidance counsellor advised her to abandon plans to study engineering because "women don't do that." She went on to work for a summer at the pulp and paper mill in Newcastle, New Brunswick, and was the first female ever to work inside. "They used to ask me where my steel-tipped high heels were, and my wire-mesh pantyhose."

As she takes me around the fragmented offices that make up TecKnowledge, she's the boss who bears the brunt of staff jokes: the engineer who still can't photocopy both sides of a page; the person in charge who is always losing crucial office keys. But clearly, her employees enjoy her and respect her. Many of them have left good jobs with established companies to work long hours (fifty to sixty per week) for TecKnowledge.

"It's really great being a woman and working for women," says business solutions manager Patti Ellis-Haddon, who's been with the company the longest, just over a year. "And I don't mean that from

a feminist point of view, but because they are aggressive and successful and inspiring."

Today their profit margin is 10 to 20 percent. Marketing and
travel costs eat up 25 percent, salaries and benefits about 50 percent, and the rest of their operating expenses go into administrative overhead. Since becoming a partner with Maritime Medical
Care, they have assembled a powerful team of nine staff employees
(mostly women). "You're expected to be assertive, to speak your
mind. You're encouraged to have opinions — or you'll be trampled!"
says Ellis-Haddon.

Spence and Weaver are trying hard to be "uncorporate" with
their staff. Everybody gets a chance to interview new applicants.
There are financial incentives for people who keep up with technical reading and training. They plan to give up 10 percent of their
own equity to offer stock options, too. And, as working mothers,
they try to accommodate personal interests and obligations.

But everyone acknowledges that Linda's own workaholic habits
are dangerous. Steps are being taken (with an incentive package)
to ensure that people do not measure their accomplishments
simply by hours worked. It's important that their staff not burn
out.

"Linda and I are the pioneers, forging ahead in search of new
products and business development," Dorothy says, summing up
the business philosophy that motivates them. "Now we have to hire
the right settlers to take over where we leave off!"

Postscript: Ryan Fudge is now thirteen years old, and Grand Manan
is a great place to explore. A few days before Christmas 1996, Ryan
and his mate Billy Bedford were snooping around some abandoned
smokehouses, once used by herring fishermen on the island. They
started to climb the long ladders up to the roof beams, thirty feet
above. Ryan lost his balance and came crashing down on the hard
dirt floor.

Somehow Ryan got up and walked away from the accident. But
this time it was his backbone that was X-rayed and transmitted to

Saint John. And telemedicine saved him yet another emergency trip over the Bay of Fundy on a wintry night.

RIDING WILDERNESS WAVES

JOYCE MAJISKI AND JILL PANGMAN

By Gail Youngberg

CATHIE ARCHBOULD

In the summer of 1996, while leading a party of canoers and rafters down the Firth River in the northern Yukon with her partner, Joyce Majiski, Jill Pangman came as close as she ever has to seriously doubting her choice of profession. They had been fighting flood conditions and strong head winds all day. It was 3:30 in the morning before they could crawl into their tents to sleep. Three hours later Pangman was awake again. A full bladder drove her out of her tent.

"I was so tired I felt sick. I couldn't focus. I was saying, 'This is ridiculous. I've just gotta find another way of making a living.' And I realized, as I was saying that, standing there just about to drop my drawers, that I was staring at a polar bear fifteen feet away. I was so tired I had not even seen it. And my first thought was, 'You didn't change your profession early enough, Pangman.'"

Pangman and Majiski are wilderness guides, co-owners of not one but two tour companies, Sila Sojourns and Ecosummer Yukon, based in Whitehorse. They lead expeditions along some of the wildest rivers in the world, in the Yukon Territory and northern British Columbia — through the canyons of the Firth River to the Beaufort Sea, through glacier country along the Alsek River in the staggeringly beautiful Kluane National Park in the southern Yukon, through the St. Elias Mountains to the Pacific Ocean along the

Tatshenshini River, wherever the adventurous are willing to hike, climb, or paddle.

Fortunately, the bear was young and more curious than hostile. While he terrified the camp, effortlessly poking his head through the screen of one tent, they were able to pack up and get out of his territory, moving very slowly and stopping to lie low each time he circled back towards them.

Jill says, "One of the things I love about this work is these really intimate moments you do have with the animals, even if some encounters seem a little close for comfort! And we've had lots of them over the years. Afterwards, it seems this is what keeps us alive and going. This is what fuels our own enthusiasm and love of this lifestyle."

Majiski and Pangman love the land itself. Joyce says, "As you visit an area again and again, there comes a feeling of familiarity that can only be described as going home. One of our favourite places is along the Alsek River valley in Kluane National Park. Climbing the flanks of Goatherd Mountain, one gets a bird's-eye view of the Lowell glacier below and close-up views of the mountain goats above. It is a place where one can be quietly awed by the power of nature."

Seeing them side by side, a stranger might take Joyce and Jill for sisters rather than business partners. They are both tall, about five foot eight, slim and very fit, dark-haired, and given to breaking out in matching grins. According to Joyce, their fitness is not acquired in a gym.

"In the winter we ski a lot. I cross-country ski almost every day, if I can. Obviously we're out all summer, and in the spring we both bicycle. I also white-water kayak and climb when I can. We're always active. It's a lifestyle. You know, you have to chop your wood, haul water."

They first met in Whitehorse in 1984. They might have been rivals, both looking for work, following the same leads around a fairly small town. But, says Joyce, "When we finally did meet we just gabbed like long-lost sisters." They found they had chosen the same university program, wildlife biology, at the University of Guelph in

Ontario, graduating three years apart (Jill in 1979, Joyce in 1982), and had followed the same track around the world, working in Australia and hiking in Nepal.

Although she hadn't planned for a career as a wilderness guide, Jill had been hoping to get back to the Yukon since her first visit in 1974 as a student assistant with conservationist and wildlife photographer Andy Russell. Pangman was then twenty years old and had lived all her life in eastern Canada, much of it near Montreal. She found the Yukon "mind boggling."

After graduating, Jill and her husband, Bruce McLean, a caribou and muskox biologist, worked on wildlife environmental and behaviour studies for a number of summers, then were overseas for three years. When they returned, Bruce got a job on Baffin Island for the summer. Unemployed, Jill flew out west. "I bought an old van and drove up to the Yukon, because I felt that was where I wanted to make my home." Bruce's work later took him to Yellowknife and then to Inuvik on the Arctic Ocean, while Jill, working as a wildlife consultant, "commuted" the length and breadth of the territories and got to know them well.

Her first job was on the Dempster Highway, between Dawson City and Inuvik, monitoring the birds of prey that were in the area and conducting naturalist excursions. She then worked with the government, the Inuit, and the Dene on a conservation plan for the western Arctic.

She loved the bush camps and the wildlife research, but she also wanted to proselytize, to see people moved by learning more about the wild environment, so she tried working with volunteer projects — the Yukon Conservation Society in Whitehorse, the Ecology North group in Yellowknife, and the National Steering Committee for the Canadian Environmental Network.

"But after two years," she says, "I finally quit the process because it got so bogged down in politics. I realized it's not really my cup of tea. What I'm much better suited to is being out on the land, because that's what I love, and being with people and sharing that. I didn't do well in the meeting scenario."

Then, in the summer of 1988, Pangman teamed up with a local guide, Martyn Williams, to put in a proposal to Parks Canada to do an interpretive guide to the Firth River, which runs through Ivvavik National Park to the Beaufort Sea. Williams and his wife, Maureen Garritty, were at that time co-owners of Ecosummer Yukon Expeditions.

"The project was a combination of an inventory, from a natural history point of view, of interpretive features in the Firth River Valley, it was to train the wardens how to raft, and it was to map all the rapids on the river. We produced a 150-page booklet on it, with some management implications and ideas for the river corridor." The next year, they published a pamphlet about the river, which appeared in 1989, with Joyce Majiski's illustrations.

After three trips on the river, one a regular guided trip conducted by Williams, and two specifically for wardens, Pangman knew that she liked guiding. The next summer she committed her whole summer to working with Williams's Ecosummer Yukon Expeditions, becoming more involved with other aspects of the business each year.

Guiding came naturally to Joyce Majiski as well. "I think guiding is a lifestyle decision that started way back when, when I was still in high school. We had an outdoors club and so I've always canoed and hiked and spent time in the wilderness. I'd been up here in 1981 and had met Maureen and Martyn, because they were living in a house with a friend of mine from university. There was a huge photograph of Bruce Cockburn and a group, on a canoe trip, and I thought, 'Well, that looks like a lot of fun. How do you start doing this?'"

While travelling in Australia, Joyce joined up with a company called Australian Himalayan Expeditions and did illustrations for their brochure in exchange for going on trips. She became an assistant guide, and when she came back to the Yukon, it seemed natural to just carry on.

"I went along as a naturalist on some trips so that was one other kind of introduction, the biology background. People want to know about the environment."

"The first few years I guided, I was really concerned about everything. I'm not sure if it had to do with the fact that I was young, and a young woman, feeling like I had to prove myself, or if it was just the immensity of the job. That feeling has dissipated with age and experience, but I'm always aware of the dangers and hazards. The white-water trips always cause the most anxiety because someone can fall out at any time — there's white water and the cold environment to think about.

"It's a twenty-four-hour-a-day job, when you're in the field. And you're everything from friend to confidante to social worker to main cook. You're having to tell people how to go to the bathroom, how to wash, how to be environmentally friendly with their water, their toothpaste, their everything. How to set up the tent, where to set up the tent. So you start off with an enormous amount of information to pass on to them, and you have to sort of allay their fears about the bears, and about a whole range of things. With women, they're always afraid, if they're having their menstruation, are the bears going to come around more. They're questions that they would ask me but they wouldn't ask a guy."

Sometimes the visitors are the show and the wildlife are the spectators. On a trip to Keale Peak in the Mackenzie mountains, Joyce remembers hanging back to photograph and "navel gaze" while Jill took the group on ahead. "As I caught up, I noticed a group of five magnificent bull caribou. This was August and the bulls were in soft velvet, although their antlers were nearly fully grown. The bulls were intent on the group, but the group were intent on a cow and calf caribou, farther up the valley. The five bulls sneaked around the humans, who lay unsuspecting and gazing into their binoculars. The people didn't notice the bulls, despite their size and proximity, until a few minutes later, and then they were caught between five bulls and a cow-calf duo! Which to watch?

"Safety is only one aspect of a very complex job," she continued. "We do the cooking, and on a rafting trip we use oar frames [a rigid frame with oarlocks that fits over the raft so that it can be rowed], so we're in control of the raft, although people can paddle. It's physically demanding, depending on what you're doing. On the hiking trips, we usually carry more weight. You have to have first aid. Jill and I both have the highest standard you can get, Advanced Wilderness First Aid, a 90- to 100-hour course. And we re-cert that every three years." Even on the relatively less demanding Sila Sojourns trips, Pangman and Majiski ask their clients to include emergency evacuation insurance in their medical coverage.

How *do* they go to the bathroom, when there is no bathroom and protecting the environment is as important as enjoying it? Joyce is uncompromising.

"We collect all the paper. We don't want people to bury paper anywhere, because it just doesn't disintegrate. On the hiking trips, we have a little plastic bag that goes out, and a trowel kit, and they dig a little hole and do what they need to do, and carry their paper back, and if it's not a walking trip (i.e., rafting), then we carry it out.

"On the rafting trips we have to carry everything out. So we have a little scat packer [plastic bucket with tight-fitting lid]. Or we use what's called a rocket box, fitted with a little seat. It's pretty private. We set up a scenic spot, off away from everyone, and downwind, and then you use a paddle system. When the paddle's up, the bathroom's available. When the paddle's down, you have to just hang on for a second."

While Jill was guiding virtually from one end of the earth to the other, Joyce was establishing herself as an artist, travelling in the off-season to printmaking and papermaking studios in Mexico, Italy, Spain, British Columbia, and the Banff Centre for the Arts in Alberta. Since 1989, her work has been shown in galleries in Vancouver and Victoria, British Columbia, as well as in Whitehorse.

"It's been an interesting juggling match," she says. "There was a period, a few years, probably in the mid-eighties, when I was going through a big crisis trying to decide whether I should be a biologist or whether I should be an artist, and I can't give up either of those."

Majiski and Pangman started Sila Sojourns in the fall of 1993. Jill says, "I was not sure about my continued involvement with Ecosummer. Joyce and I had both been guiding that style of trip for a while — the traditional adventure tours and travel — and we both felt that we really wanted our own creation, that had more of a creative focus, and more time incorporated into the trips for inspiration and quietness."

Sila (pronounced "seelah") is an Inuit word for nature and free-spiritedness that signifies the life-giving force. "It embodies the philosophy of Sila Sojourns," Jill says. "What drove us to do this is very much our love of being out there and our desire to share that with people. It wasn't as a way to make a good buck." Joyce agrees. "It's really difficult to separate where the business ends and where our life begins."

Over the winter of 1993–94, Pangman and Majiski wrote a brochure, illustrated with Pangman's stunning photos of the landscape and Majiski's sketches. They sent it out to women's networks and to writers' and arts groups and advertised in newsletters where they thought it might attract the kind of people they were interested in. Their first Sila trip was to be an all-women's sea-kayaking tour of Atlin Lake, a glacial lake along the British Columbia–Yukon border. Jill put together a slide show, and eventually ten women participated, half from Whitehorse and half from elsewhere. They finished that season of Sila Sojourns trips with a writing retreat at a fly-in lodge on Primrose Lake in the southern Yukon.

In the meantime, Martyn Williams offered to sell Ecosummer Yukon Expeditions to Jill for $10,000. She realized it was a very good deal. The equipment alone was worth that, in spite of the hard use it had seen, and in addition she would be getting the name of the company, a client list and marketing, through the main Ecosummer Canada office in Vancouver.

Moving from just guiding to total responsibility didn't seem like much of a jump actually, according to Joyce. "Jill and I were the main guides for the company. Jill was managing it at that point, and I was helping her to make a lot of decisions. It seemed like a very natural progression to buy Martyn out." Joyce put $3,000 of her savings into the business when she joined it in the second year.

In spite of the low start-up cost, it wasn't easy. "That first summer," Joyce says, "I think we made $3,000 profit. We barely made wages, but we didn't lose money." They did all of the Sila Sojourns trips themselves and hired six guides over the course of the summer to help out with Ecosummer Yukon bookings.

And they kept their personal costs at rock bottom. Jill and Bruce were house-sitting at a friend's place, with no electricity and no phone. Joyce was living in a cabin at the other end of Whitehorse, half an hour away. They had a telephone-answering service in town and used their own vehicles, leasing a van when they needed one.

"I probably live on less money than most people," Joyce says. "I've been living in a cabin most of the time I've been up here. I've been in the same place for about nine years, and my rent was $300 a month. I shared it with different friends over the years, and in the winter, when I was away, I would sublet it. So, pretty cheap, actually."

In the 1996 season, their profit was more than $10,000, in spite of having put nearly $15,000 into new equipment. Expenses are always high. In the vast distances of the territories, a large part of the high fees paid by clients — between $2,000 and $3,500 for a ten- to twelve-day trip — goes on air charter fees. Inventory includes five eighteen-foot rafts, two sixteen-footers and one fifteen-footer, and a wide assortment of tents. They rent sea kayaks and canoes from a friend in the business when they're needed. Joyce says, "Every year we try to upgrade the gear just a little bit more. The worst thing is to get out to the Firth River and realize you've taken the wrong tent, the one with the screen door that's all ripped up, and it's in the middle of mosquito season and people are just going crazy. You just can't do that."

Jill and Joyce each did seven trips in the 1996 season. They prefer working together, according to Jill, but it's not always possible.

"We're slowly trying to train more people and give them more natural history background. A lot of people who live in this area are real outdoor people. And also there's a lot of companies that are about the same age as ours. So we just mix and match.

"I'm not sure that we would do that for outside companies. There's different kinds of ethics. If people are similar to us and we know that they would run the trip the way we would, then we might as well pass the business on. Otherwise, we both lose out. People spread the word. And they'll come back."

When I talked to them in January 1997, Joyce was in Whitehorse, already planning the next season and weighing equipment needs against last year's profit. Jill was in Montreal, visiting with family and wondering whether they could stretch the budget to cover an extra person to manage the office.

She reflects, "We've had to do it all, because we've started it from limited finances. We've slowly been able to build it up, and we don't have any debts with it. All of our equipment is paid for and we have enough to keep it going year to year. We pay ourselves for the trips we work on, for the days we pack food, for packing equipment, or driving, if we're driving a group out, and if we're working on a trip." As the business grows, however, it's become apparent that there's a gap in their arrangements: "We don't pay ourselves for the office."

Temporarily away from the books and the year-end accounting, she says, "I start to wonder if it might be a good idea to get someone involved who has a lot of strong skills at marketing."

Both of them know that they are facing burn-out if they don't ease up on themselves. The adventure treks that are the mainstay of the Ecosummer tours are physically very demanding. "Certainly there's been the odd moment," Jill says, "when I've been rowing a raft out to the Beaufort Sea into a head wind and thinking, I don't want to be doing this thirty years from now.

"We've had to push ourselves a little more than we might have otherwise, just because we've had to make sure that Ecosummer still works, and we have a responsibility to those clients and Ecosummer in Vancouver, not to put it on the back burner. But we want Sila to go, so we've been pulled between the two. We've been focusing the last two summers on slowly getting more people hired that we can trust to do the Ecosummer trips, so we can be freed up for the Sila work."

In the meantime, Jill and her husband have been able to buy some land and build a house on it, and Joyce has bought a cabin and moved it over to their site.

In the year 2000, perhaps, they will be able to take the summer off, to see where they are. "I think," Jill concludes, "that we see Sila as something we'll probably always want to hold for as long as we can imagine, because it can grow and change as we do and fill the needs in ourselves and what we see as a need in the kinds of clients that we get."

AFTERWORD
HOW TO SUCCEED IN
BUSINESS BY REALLY TRYING

When we chose the women to profile in *Taking Care of Business,* we tried to find as wide a variety as possible, but in spite of their personal differences, as businesswomen they turn out to have a lot in common. These similarities are worth remembering. They include:

- A bright idea that fills a need

- Drive, energy, and physical stamina

- Charisma, chutzpah, a personal touch

- Common sense

- A sense of humour

- A gift for marketing and organizing

- A talent for partnerships

Perhaps the most important trait these women share is a sense of timing. Success in business requires a creative instinct — journalists call it a "nose for news" — that makes other people sit up and say, "Gee, why didn't I think of that?" Don't imitate, innovate. New opportunities are constantly appearing, and some of the best may be those closest to home. Here are three examples:

1. THE NICHE MARKET

In 1968, Judy Sarick of Toronto was living in London, England. A specialist in children's literature, both as a librarian and a university teacher, Sarick began to haunt the London stores for books to entertain her two-year-old daughter, Tema. "I found I couldn't get out of a store spending less than about $200 in today's money," Sarick laughs. In 1974, after she had returned to Canada as head of school libraries for the Toronto Board of Education, she was invited to a children's birthday party at the home of wealthy friends.

"I took some new books I'd received from the publishers. Everyone was so excited! 'Where did you get them?' They had never seen books like these, and I realized that nobody in Canada had properly tried to sell them."

Sarick opened The Children's Book Store on Avenue Road near Bloor Street that September. "I wanted to be in Yorkville," she laughs, "but I couldn't afford it. All the publishers tried to talk me out of it. They said it was a big mistake, but I figured if I could sell $100 worth of books a year to 600 families I'd make it."

A week after Sarick's store opened, poet Dennis Lee published his phenomenally popular book of children's verse, *Alligator Pie*. "I'd ordered 250 copies," Sarick says. "The book sold out in weeks, and I was the only store with stock." In her first year, she did double the business she'd anticipated.

Sarick's timing was perfect, and she did three things right:

- She opened her store close to a major tourist area that featured specialty shops, affluent buyers, and a year-round family attraction, the Royal Ontario Museum.

- She understood her market: well-educated working mothers with money to spend and guilty feelings about not staying at home. These women were ambitious for their kids, and nostalgic for the beautiful books they had read as children in a pre-television era.

- She realized that her market was sophisticated, discriminating, and small. Sarick refuses to sell the mass-market "schlock" that can be found in discount stores and supermarkets, and she is resigned to the fact that a lot of Toronto parents will never hear about her store. Instead, she has concentrated on sales to schools and libraries, mail order, and boosting her walk-in retail traffic. In 1993, The Children's Book Store moved from downtown to North Toronto, an upscale area near schools and family-oriented stores that attract customers from all over the city. "I hit the last of the baby boom," Sarick says, "and now I'm getting the echo."

2. ABORIGINAL OPPORTUNITIES

The explosion of world-wide demand for native North American arts and crafts is providing unique opportunities for aboriginal merchants. One of their leaders is Nancy Nightingale, owner of Khot-La-Cha, a North Vancouver shop specializing in original, high-quality Coast Salish handicrafts. Eight years ago, Nightingale, who had worked for fifteen years for B.C. Telephone, bought the business from her mother, Emily Baker.

Baker, whose husband, Simon, is chief of the Squamish Nation, started selling the work of local carvers from a small store she had built next to the family home in 1969. "It was mostly word of mouth," she recalls. "A lot of people would come back, and bring their friends from Europe." Located a short block south of Marine Drive on the way to the scenic Capilano Canyon, Khot-La-Cha was one of the first Indian-owned enterprises to gain a share of the lucrative tourist trade, and Nightingale has expanded her stock to include the work of West Coast painters and silversmiths as well as Iroquois masks and Ojibwa moccasins from Ontario. Since Khot-La-Cha is located on Indian land, Baker and Nightingale pay no taxes on their property, profits, or income from the store.

Nightingale cautions, however, that being on reserve land is not necessarily an advantage: "When I wanted to buy my mother out, I was refused a loan by an organization that funds native business. They said the transaction was not 'arm's length,' but I felt it was only fair that my mother should be compensated for the years of work she had put into the store." Nightingale, who has Indian status but is married to a non-native, lives off the reserve, and she took out a second mortgage on her house to finance a bank loan.

"If I had lived on the reserve, I couldn't have gotten that mortgage," she says. "Banks won't touch reserve property. There is no encouragement for native people to go into business, even though we *can* do these things!"

Nightingale has a business college education and experience in both accounting and customer service. "My goal was to make some spending money," she laughs. "Within two years, I was making three times my income at B.C. Tel, and it's gone up from there."

In 1995, Aboriginal Business Canada, an arm of Industry Canada, sponsored Nightingale to attend a trade show of aboriginal arts and crafts in Frankfurt, Germany, and the following year, it paid half her costs to become an exhibitor. She is grateful for the publicity and exposure, but wary about relying too much on government assistance.

"Funding organizations demand so much from you," she says. "There is so much paperwork!"

Nightingale sells at two trade shows in the United States every year and promotes her business by joining numerous local aboriginal, women's, tourist, and business organizations. In terms of recognition, her big break was being runner-up in the "Quality Plus" category as Canadian Woman Entrepreneur of the Year in 1994. She is expanding her store, and spending more time doing workshops with young natives, many of them artists, who want to go into business for themselves. "Don't run out of stock," she advises them, "and keep a hand on your cash flow!"

3. THE MULTICULTURAL MARKET

With our diversity of population, Canada is full of business opportunities for people who can fulfil specific needs. Among the most urgent of these needs is to look attractive, and until Beverly Mascoll went into the hair-care and cosmetics business in Toronto in 1970, that was a big problem for black women like her. In Canada, products designed for Caucasian women didn't suit their skin colouring, hair texture or fashion sense, and American products were hard to come by.

Mascoll, a professional beautician, started selling hair relaxers out of the trunk of her car. She was in business full time when a huge wave of immigrants from the West Indies hit Toronto, and black became beautiful. These women didn't have a great deal of money to spend on themselves, but they would scrimp on other things to buy cosmetics and have their hair done.

Ethnic products are now one of the fastest-growing areas of the multi-billion-dollar beauty market, and with 3,000 products and five Toronto retail stores, Mascoll Beauty Supply Ltd. is thriving in a competitive field. A long-time activist in the black community, Mascoll, with twenty-one other women, recently established the Beverly Mascoll Community Foundation to assist needy women and children of all races. Now in her fifties, she has no intention of selling or retiring. She told Margaret Cannon of the *Globe and Mail*'s *Report on Business* magazine, "Our biggest challenges are ahead of us."

There is no formula for success — if there were, we'd all be rich! The advice most businesswomen give is simple, and it boils down to a slogan my mother used to repeat to me until it was burned into my brain: "Make the most of what you have." These words have given me a lot of confidence, but if you're looking for more specific, hands-on help, there are plenty of sources.

- Your local chamber of commerce, board of trade, or provincial departments of industry and commerce. Small business is a growth area, and some of these organizations may have programs geared to encouraging women.

- Universities, community and commercial colleges, and night schools offer a variety of courses in all aspects of accounting, financial planning, and business management.

Women entrepreneurs have become organized, so you may want to give these people a call:

Canadian Association of Women Executives and Entrepreneurs, #300 - 595 Bay St., Toronto, ON M5G 2C2.
Phone: (416) 482-2933. Fax: (416) 596-7894

Canadian Federation of Business and Professional Women's Clubs, #308 - 56 Sparks St., Ottawa, ON K1P 5A9.
Phone and fax: (613) 234-7619

Women Entrepreneurs of Canada, #1200 - 390 Bay St. Toronto, ON M5H 2Y2. Phone: (416) 860-1125. Fax: (416) 860-1188.

If you live in Newfoundland, there is the Women's Enterprise Bureau, 30 Harvey Rd., St. John's, NF A1C 2G1.
Phone: (709) 754-5555. Fax: (709) 754-0079.

In British Columbia, contact the Western Businesswomen's Association, #302 - 1107 Homer St., Vancouver, BC V6B 2Y1.
Phone: (604) 688-0951. Fax: (604) 681-4545.

The Alberta Women's Enterprise Initiative Association has two offices, one in Calgary, Alberta, at #260 - 800 6th Ave. S.W. T2P 3G3, and the other in Edmonton at #100 - 10237 104th St. N.W. T5J 1B1. The toll-free phone number is 1-800-713-3558.

Programs and organizations come and go, but these contacts will be able to refer you to others closer to home or more related to your interests. Good luck, and good business!

AUTHOR BIOGRAPHIES

Margot Brunelle   Margot Brunelle is from Montreal and started her journalism career at CBC-TV in Toronto. She ran away to Halifax in 1979 and has worked as a freelance writer, producer, and broadcaster (for CBC Radio). Married with three sons, she considers herself a qualified "circus-performer," who specializes in juggling (kids, career, money, and madness!).

Liane Faulder   Liane Faulder is a city columnist with the *Edmonton Journal.* Her writing background features extensive experience in women's issues, including a 1991 National Newspaper Award nomination for a series on new birth technologies. "Telling women's stories has always been a passion for me," says Faulder. "I chose Eveline Charles and Gail Hall for profiles because I was fascinated, in both cases, to see how less-than-auspicious beginnings can nevertheless lead to solid business success later in life."

A graduate of Ryerson Polytechnic University in Toronto and the mother of two school-age boys, Faulder's career has also included stints as a researcher and story editor for CBC radio and television.

Jane Harris   Jane Harris writes about entrepreneurs and her articles have appeared in many publications, including *Price Costco Connection, Home Business Report, Alberta Venture,* and *Head Office at Home.* She undertakes historical research projects — one of her interests is the role of southern Alberta women in turn-of-the-century social reform — and has been involved in organizing political tours and fund-raising dinners. Jane is working on her second university degree, in business administration, and is the single mother of three children.

Rosa Harris-Adler   Rosa Harris-Adler, winner of a National Magazine Award in 1996, has been a freelance writer and editor since 1980. A generalist, she has written on everything from baby food to global economics but particularly enjoys doing profiles.

Diane Luckow   Diane Luckow is a Burnaby, British Columbia, journalist who freelances full-time for a variety of corporate and publishing clients. She works primarily for Toronto-based publications and has never actually met most of the editors with whom she works. Much of her workday is spent on the telephone, interviewing far-flung Canadians about their lives and businesses.

A writer for the past fifteen years, she'll tackle any topic with the exception of politics, sports, and science. Over the years, her byline has appeared in such publications as the *Globe and Mail, Maclean's, Chatelaine, Profit,* the *Financial Times,* the *Financial Post, Equinox, Flare,* and many more.

Laura Pratt

Laura Pratt is a Toronto-based freelance writer with a special interest in women's issues and entrepreneurial success stories. As a four-year veteran of the universe of the self-employed, Laura found herself nodding a lot in recognition over the course of her interviews for these profiles.

Helen Stein

Helen Stein heads her own communications business — EasyWriters — providing writing, editing, and desktop publishing services to corporate clients. Her byline also appears in a number of Canadian magazines and newspapers. She lives in Winnipeg with her husband, Paul, and enjoys travelling, watercolour painting, and spending time with her family.

Kathryn Welbourn

Kathryn Welbourn is a freelance writer, researcher, and broadcaster living in Portugal Cove, Newfoundland. Her work has appeared in national magazines — including *Harrowsmith* and *Chatelaine* — in newspapers, and on CBC Radio. In 1996, she won a silver medal at the National Magazine Awards for her first full feature article, "Outports and Outlaws," which was pubished by *Equinox.*

When asked to contribute to this book, Welbourn immediately thought of Dolores Tobin. "I admire her determination to stay in the home she loves, and everyone at my house loves her butter."

Gail Youngberg   Gail Youngberg grew up in mining towns in northern Quebec and northern Ontario, and took degrees in English at the universities of Toronto and Saskatchewan. She has been writing and teaching in and about Saskatchewan for many years, is a former editor of *NeWest Review*, and is a long-standing member of the *Herstory* calendar collective. She is married, has two sons, and currently lives in Saskatoon.